BEN M. SCHORR

Microsoft
Office 365
for Lawyers

D1570020

A PRACTICAL GUIDE TO OPTIONS
AND IMPLEMENTATION

ABALAW
PRACTICE
DIVISION
The Business of Practicing Law

Cover design by RIPE Creative, Inc.

Library of Congress Cataloging-in-Publication Data

Schorr, Ben M., author.
 Microsoft Office 365 for lawyers / Ben M. Schorr.
    pages cm
 Includes bibliographical references and index.
 ISBN 978-1-62722-848-0 (alk. paper)
 1. Microsoft Office. 2. Law offices--United States--Automation. 3. Web services--United States. I. Title.
 KF320.A9S367 2014
 005.5--dc23

                              2014027247

Dedication

For Tom Mighell, without whose leadership and feedback this book probably never would have happened.

Contents

About the Author

Ben M. Schorr is a technologist and Chief Executive Officer for Roland Schorr & Tower, a professional consulting firm headquartered in Honolulu, Hawaii with offices in Los Angeles, California and Flagstaff, Arizona. In that capacity, he consults with a wide variety of organizations, including many law firms. He is frequently sought as a writer, teacher, and speaker for groups as diverse as the Hawaii Visitor and Convention Bureau, Microsoft, and the American Bar Association. More than 18 years ago, Microsoft named him as an MVP in their Outlook product group and he has been supporting Outlook, Exchange, Office 365, and most recently OneNote ever since.

Prior to co-founding Roland Schorr, he was the Director of Information Services for Damon Key Leong Kupchak Hastert, a large Honolulu law firm, for almost 8 years.

Mr. Schorr has been a technical editor or contributor on a number of other books over the years. For several years he was half of the "Ask the Exchange Pros" team for *Windows Server System* magazine. He is the author of *The Lawyer's Guide to*

Microsoft Outlook 2013 and *The Lawyer's Guide to Microsoft Word 2010*, published by the American Bar Association.

In October of 2005, Mr. Schorr was named by the Pacific Technology Foundation as one of the Top 50 Technology Leaders in Hawaii. He's a member of the Institute of Electrical and Electronics Engineers' (IEEE) Computer Society, the American Bar Association, and the United States Naval Institute.

In his free time, Mr. Schorr enjoys coaching football, reading, playing softball, cooking and is a marathoner and Ironman triathlete. He currently lives in Flagstaff, Arizona with his wife Carrie, dog Sampson, and the cats who keep them around.

You can reach him at bens@rolandschorr.com.

Chapter 1

Introduction

Possibly no book I've ever written has been as loudly demanded as this one. When Microsoft launched Office 365 in June of 2011, lawyers were curious. Today solo, small, and midsized firms are flocking to it in droves, and even some of the larger firms are giving it a look as their legacy systems age.

In this book, I'm going to try to explain what Office 365 is today and answer some of the common questions that lawyers ask me when they're considering whether they should migrate their firms to Office 365. I'll also offer some guidance on how to properly set up and manage Office 365 and even offer an entire chapter with information on how to migrate to Office 365.

Office 365 is a very wide and very deep topic, and it changes so quickly that it's not really practical for me to try to write a comprehensive 800-page book; by the time I got to page 240, half of the things would probably have changed. So I've opted to make this book a little more timely and get it out a little more quickly and focus on what I think is important. The trade-off is that I can't cover every Office 365 topic in depth.

So What the Heck Is Office 365?

Well, that seems to be the magic question and, unfortunately, the answer will take more than a paragraph. At a very basic level, Office 365 is a subscription-based service from Microsoft, which offers access to a variety of software and services. Office 365 evolved out of an older, and far less well-received product called **Business Productivity Online Suite**, which was rather tragically abbreviated to "BPOS."

The software ranges from tools you're very familiar with, such as Microsoft Office, which includes **Word**, **Outlook**, and **OneNote**, to things you may not be as familiar with—like **Microsoft Visio**. The services include industry powerhouses like **Microsoft Exchange** and **SharePoint** alongside lesser-known offerings like **Microsoft CRM** and **Yammer**.

The software is installed as a **Click-to-Run** installation, which means that rather than installing from a DVD or even a traditional download, in most cases the software is installed by streaming it from the Internet. People commonly misunderstand; they think that Click-to-Run means the software is web-based (like Google Docs) or that they always have to be connected to the Internet to use it. Office 2013 via Office 365 (yes, I know it gets confusing) is installed on your local hard drive just like your current version of Microsoft Office probably is. The differences are

There are both professional and home versions of Office 365. Since this book is written for attorneys and law firms, I'm going to primarily focus on the Professional versions here.

that Office software installed through Office 365 will periodically check in with Microsoft to make sure your subscription is still active, and Microsoft will frequently push updates and even new features to you. This also means that you don't have to worry about keeping track of installation DVDs in case you ever need to reinstall the software. As long as the Internet is available, your installation files are available.

We'll talk more about Microsoft Office in Chapter 3.

The services are hosted in **The Cloud** at Microsoft's data centers. We'll talk more about the main services in detail in later chapters but here's a quick summary:

- **Exchange Server (Chapter 4).** This is Microsoft's enterprise-class groupware server for e-mail, calendar, contacts, tasks, and more. In addition to syncing to Microsoft Outlook for PC or Mac, it also syncs to virtually every mobile device (smartphones or tablets) and has a very good web-mail client too. Most of the Fortune 500 and virtually all of the AmLaw 100 use Microsoft Exchange server. Thanks to Office 365, it's no longer out of reach for even solo firms, and it's one of the best reasons to choose Office 365.

- **SharePoint (Chapter 5).** This is Microsoft's collaboration, document and workflow platform. With SharePoint, firms can create document libraries, shared calendars, project lists, and more. SharePoint "team sites" can be shared within your firm or even used to create extranets that you share with clients, co-counsel, experts, or others. You can even create and host your firm's public website in SharePoint.

- **Lync (Chapter 6).** This is Microsoft's secure communications platform. It does instant messaging, voice and video calling, and even screen-sharing and white-boarding. You can have multi-party Lync calls—handy if you want to have a meeting with multiple people in different locations. In addition to the locally installed and mobile clients for Lync, there is also a web client for Lync that works in a browser. With it, you can have Lync calls with people who don't have a Lync client installed. I have clients who have used that feature to host webinars for clients or prospective clients.

- **Dynamics CRM.** Customer Relationship Management (CRM) is a hot topic in business and certainly in law. While many firms use their practice management software as a CRM tool, others prefer to use a dedicated CRM platform. Microsoft offers Dynamics CRM as a way for companies to keep track of their marketing efforts, plan and track communications with customers or potential customers, and try to coordinate the entire client lifecycle.

Since very few of the Office 365 plans that attorneys care about include Dynamics CRM, and I don't want this to turn into 600 pages, I'm not going to devote a lot of time to it in this book.

A Subscription Model?

Many folks are pushing back on the subscription model of software. Most of us are used to paying $399, one time, and then using that software forever. Sometimes we didn't even realize we were paying the $399 because our software was bundled with our computer, and the cost was just quietly rolled in. I'll admit that at first I wasn't too keen on the subscription idea either. But Microsoft has done a couple of things to sweeten the deal.

First of all, they've kept the pricing relatively low. For most software, it will take at least two years of subscription costs to equal the cost of that box of software. Secondly, many of the plans bundle in some valuable services. When you consider what those services are worth, the package becomes considerably better. And finally, they've been quite liberal with the licensing. You may be paying $12 a month for Microsoft Office, but that $12 a month lets you install Office not just on the PC on your desk, but also on the laptop in your bag and the Mac at your house and the iPad you're carrying around and...pretty soon you're effectively paying just $3 or $4 per month per device. At that price, it could be *eight or ten years* before you'll have spent as much money in the subscription plan as you would have with the boxed software.

We'll talk more about Microsoft's licensing model in the next chapter, but it's important to know that with the Office 365 plans, you can generally add—or remove—users one at a time whenever you need to. That means that you don't have to buy a ten-pack of licenses if you only need eight today. Buy eight. When you hire an additional staffer, you can add another license. If somebody leaves your firm and you're not immediately replacing that person, you can reduce your license count—and your monthly expenses.

Do I Really Need to Upgrade?

Well, *need* is a strong word. When it comes to Office 2013, I answer that question this way:

If you have	then you
Office 2010	probably don't need to upgrade to 2013 right away
Office 2007	probably should upgrade to 2013 right away
Office 2003 (or an older version)	should definitely upgrade to 2013

As for the services, Microsoft Exchange server is the crown jewel in the Office 365 crown, and if you're currently using a **POP3** or **IMAP-based** e-mail system (especially if you're using an @yahoo.com or @gmail.com address for your firm), then you should definitely step up to a professional e-mail system with hosted Exchange.

Whether you're going to use SharePoint or Lync is a question you'll need to think hard about. Some firms use those services very successfully, but they might not fit into your workflow. Chapters 5 and 6 will talk more specifically about those, and hopefully you'll have a good feel for whether SharePoint and/or Lync will work for your firm after you've read those.

What You Need to Know

With Microsoft Office 365, you select a set of software products and services, and you pay a monthly subscription fee that ranges from $4 to $24 or so per mailbox. The services are delivered to you via The Cloud, and the software is locally installed just as your software traditionally has been. This is the direction that Microsoft is heading towards for all of its software distribution.

One other thing you really need to know about this entire book: it is about a very dynamic software product. By the time I've finished typing this sentence, it's possible that Microsoft will have changed something about the product. So you may want to hear "as of this writing" in your head before most of the paragraphs in this book.

Chapter 2

Getting Office 365

Getting Office 365 for your firm is a little different from how you traditionally bought software. In all likelihood you're not going to run down to Best Buy and come back to the office with a box of Office 365. The majority of companies buying Office 365 do so online, often (but not necessarily) with the help of a Microsoft Partner.

Since there are quite a few different kinds of Office 365, the first step is giving some thought to which plan you need.

It's All about the Mailbox

When you're considering Office 365, one of the most important things to know is that most Office 365 plans are priced not by the user or by the device but by the mailbox (see Figure 2.1). Generally speaking, especially in law firms, the mailbox tends to map fairly closely to the user. Each user tends to have his or her own mailbox, even though a considerable number of mailboxes may be shared—such as when a legal assistant has access to an attorney's calendar.

Figure 2.1   Mailboxes

However, users with a single mailbox may have multiple computers or devices, such as the attorney who has a desktop PC on her desk, a laptop in her bag, an Android tablet in her purse, and a Mac at home. In that case, Office 365 considers that just a single mailbox—not a user with four devices (see Figure 2.2).

Also, a single mailbox may have multiple e-mail addresses (referred to as **aliases**). Your firm administrator may have hisname@yourfirmname.com and hr@yourfirmname.com, but that's still just one mailbox. It's also possible that you have staff who share a single mailbox. One firm I worked at had three messengers on staff, but they all shared a single mailbox called messengers@thatfirm.com, which they accessed from a couple of different PCs and their individual smartphones. For Office 365 purposes, that would be one mailbox, not three users, or multiple computers and smartphones (see Figure 2.3).

Figure 2.2   Multiple Devices But Still Just One Mailbox

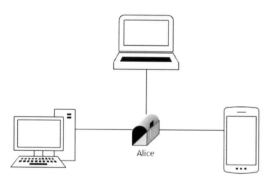

Figure 2.3   Multiple Aliases But Still Just One Mailbox

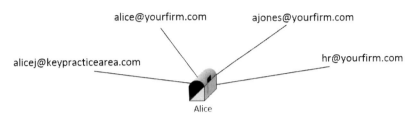

So when you're figuring out your costs of Office 365, it's most important to understand how many actual mailboxes you're going to use.

Which Office 365 Is for You?

The next question you're going to have to answer is which **SKU** (version) of Office 365 you want.

> *SKU*, as you may know if you have any experience in retail, stands for Stock Keeping Unit which is just an inventory term used to differentiate different products. The number of SKUs that a store stocks is merely a count of how many different products it stocks. When it comes to Office 365, the number of SKUs is a count of how many different varieties of Office 365 are offered.

Versions of Office 365 may be software only, services only, or a combination of the two. Interestingly enough, some versions of Office 365 don't actually include Office. At last count there were at least forty-one different SKUs of Office 365, but realistically only about half a dozen are versions that most lawyers will care about, so I'll focus on those in this book.

Another important thing to know is that there are three families of Office 365 software: Small Business, Midsize Business, and

Enterprise. You can mix and match licenses from within a family—for example, you can have five seats of Small Business and three seats of Small Business Premium but you can't easily mix and match between families. So you can't have nine seats of Small Business and five seats of Midsize Business—at least not unless you want two completely separate subscriptions that don't talk to each other.

Does Your Plan Include Office?

ProPlus	Yes
Small Business	No
Small Business Premium	Yes
Midsize Business	Yes
K1 (Kiosk)	No
Exchange-Only	No
E1	No
E3	Yes
E4	Yes

Also, until recently, you couldn't move easily between families. So if you bought Small Business and later needed to upgrade to Midsize Business, there wasn't an easy way to do that. Thankfully Microsoft has rectified that situation and made it easy to move *up* in family (from Small to Midsize to Enterprise) but you still can't go the other way—there's currently no easy way to downgrade from Enterprise to Midsize to Small.

> In fact, as of this writing, if you want to move down to a plan from a "smaller" family, you have to pull all of your data out of the Office 365 services, cancel your current plan, spin up a brand new plan in the new family, and then push all of your data back in. We've done that for clients on a couple of occasions. While it is doable, it's not fun, easy, or cheap.

Your decision about which family to choose should be guided by the families' primary distinguishing feature—the number of users it supports.

- The **Small Business** family of plans support firms with up to 25 mailboxes. If you're a small firm with ten users, Small Business may be a good choice for you.

- The **Midsize Business** family of plans support firms with up to 300 mailboxes. That covers the vast majority of firms who would consider Office 365; however, this family has only a single plan right now, and it's not a great fit for everybody. So, many firms that are comfortable in the Midsize range have opted for Enterprise plans anyhow because those plans were a better fit.

- The **Enterprise** family of plans support an unlimited number of users and mailboxes. Companies like Toyota and the American Red Cross have tens of thousands of users on Office 365 Enterprise plans. That said, one of the most attractive plans for small law firms is in the Enterprise family because it can be the least expensive way to get Office 365 if all you want is hosted Exchange Server. I have clients running just one or two users on Enterprise plans too. The takeaway there is that while the families may have a maximum number of users they support, there is no minimum.

So let's take a more detailed look at some of the Office plans that you might be interested in.

Exchange Only

If you're happy with the version of Microsoft Office that you have (and it's at least Office 2007) but you want to step up to a professional e-mail system like Microsoft Exchange as inexpensively as possible, you might opt for the Exchange Only Plan. Even though it is the least expensive of the plans lawyers tend to care about ($4 per mailbox per month), it is actually part of the Enterprise family of plans. This is the plan that even many solo and small firms choose because it gives them the power of Exchange server at an almost inconsequential price.

This plan can also be a good choice for firms that have an aging on-premises Exchange server and who are wrestling with the question of whether to upgrade it or not.

With the Exchange Only plan you get 50GB Exchange mailboxes that can synchronize to PCs, Macs, smartphones, tablets, and just about everything. (We'll talk more about Exchange server in Chapter 4.)

You can use your own **domain name** (yourfirmname.com). In fact, you can have multiple domain names at no extra charge (other than the approximately $10 per year per domain name that you pay your domain registrar). That means that you can have you@yourfirmname.com and you@yourpracticearea.com and you@yourstatelaw.com and... just about as many domain names as you happen to own and want e-mail addresses for.

Office 365 also lets you add a practically unlimited number of e-mail addresses to each mailbox. So you can have you@yourf-irmname.com and practicearea@yourfirmname.com and jobs@ yourfirmname.com and any other aliases where you might want to receive e-mail.

One of our clients has a very difficult to spell name. So in addition to toughname@herfirm.com she also has tuff-name@herfirm.com and tuffnaim@herfirm.com so that when people use the common misspellings of her name she'll still receive the mail. All of her outgoing mail (even replies to the misspellings) goes out under toughname@herfirm.com so hopefully people eventually learn the correct spelling. It doesn't cost her any extra to have those additional aliases.

As I mentioned earlier in this chapter, pricing is by the mailbox, not by the e-mail address, device, or user.

You can use Outlook 2007 or later to connect to these mailboxes, and you can connect to them from virtually any modern smartphone or tablet on the market, and there is also a very good web-based e-mail client included called Outlook Web Access, or OWA (see Figure 2.4).

Figure 2.4 Outlook Web Access

As I'll discuss in more depth in Chapter 4, Exchange offers more than e-mail. With Exchange you also get calendaring, contacts, and tasks—all of which will sync to multiple devices fairly seamlessly.

The Exchange Only plan (which also goes by the name Exchange Online Plan 1), as its name suggests, is just Exchange. It is a great choice for firms who (1) are currently using POP3/IMAP servers, (2) are unhappy with

Some older smartphones will sync e-mail, calendar, and contacts just fine but may struggle to sync tasks. Newer smartphones get the tasks as well, and there are third-party applications that even can sync tasks on the older phones.

the reliability or synchronization, (3) already have a version of Microsoft Office they're happy with, and (4) don't want or need SharePoint or Lync. At $4 per mailbox per month, it's almost a no-brainer.

Small Business

If you're a firm with fewer than twenty-five mailboxes and you want to have Exchange, SharePoint, and Lync but you don't need to upgrade to a newer version of Microsoft Office, then you might like the Small Business plan. It includes 50 GB Exchange mailboxes just like the Exchange Only plan, but it also includes SharePoint, OneDrive for Business, and Lync.

Each user gets 25GB of **OneDrive for Business** Cloud storage, which can be shared with other users both inside and outside your organization. The amount of SharePoint space you get is a bit trickier to explain. You get a base of 10GB plus you get 500MB more per user. So if you have ten users you would get 10GB of base plus 5GB of additional storage (10 users x 500MB) for a total of 15GB. If you have five users you'd get 10GB plus 2.5GB of additional storage for a total of 12.5GB. With one user you'd get 10GB plus 500MB for a total of 10.5GB. Hopefully that clears it up a bit.

Small Business is priced at $6 per mailbox per month if you pay it monthly, but if you pay the whole year in advance, you get a discount that drops the price to only $5 per mailbox per month—or $60 per mailbox per year.

Small Business Premium

The Small Business Premium plan is essentially the same as the Small Business plan, though with one major addition. You still get the 50GB Exchange mailboxes, 25GB of OneDrive for each user, 10GB (plus 500MB per user) of SharePoint and Lync as you do with Small Business. The Premium part means that you also get the latest version of Microsoft Office on up to five devices per user.

We'll talk more about Microsoft Office in Chapter 3, but for now you need to know that it includes:

- Word
- Excel
- OneNote
- Outlook
- PowerPoint
- Publisher
- Access

These are the full locally installed applications, though, as we'll see in Chapter 3, they are installed (and updated) from the Internet. The license you get for Office allows each user to install it on a primary machine—like the desktop at the office—but also on up to four additional computers, such as one or more laptops and/or machines at home. Also it's cross-platform, which means you can install it on PCs and Macs.

The current version of Office for PCs is Microsoft Office 2013. The current version of Office for Macs is Microsoft Office 2011. The Office 365 Small Business Premium license allows you to install either version as appropriate.

Not only is Office available to you on the PC or Mac, but if you have Small Business Premium you also have licenses for the **Office Mobile** apps such as **Microsoft Word for iPad**.

The Small Business Premium plan can be a great choice if you have fewer than twenty-five mailboxes (remember, it is part of the Small Business family) and you want Exchange, SharePoint, and/or Lync and you also want to upgrade to the latest version of Microsoft Office.

Small Business Premium is currently priced at $15 per mailbox per month, but you get a very attractive discount if you pay the full year in advance. The price drops to $12.50 per mailbox per month or $150 per mailbox per year. That's $30 per year per mailbox—cheaper than paying the month-to- month rate!

Note that a thirty-day free trial is available for the Small Business Premium package in case you want to try it out before you break out the credit card.

Midsize Business

If you like the sound of the Small Business Premium plan but you've got more than twenty-five mailboxes (but fewer than 300), the Midsize Business plan may be just your ticket. Like Small Business Premium, the Midsize Business plan includes 50GB Exchange mailboxes, 25GB of OneDrive for Business Cloud storage for each user, 10GB of SharePoint (plus 500MB per user), Lync, and the full suite of Microsoft Office.

One small difference in this plan is that the Microsoft Office suite you get also includes Microsoft InfoPath. It is an electronic forms application that Microsoft recently announced it would be discontinuing and replacing with an as-of-yet unannounced product. InfoPath is one of those products that seems like it would have been popular with law firms, especially firms practicing in high-volume consumer practice areas, but it never really caught on. Since you're probably not using InfoPath either you probably don't care too much that it's included with Midsize Business.

Another difference in the Midsize Business plan compared to the Small Business plans is that Midsize Business includes **Active Directory** integration. That means that if you have an on-premises Windows Server environment that includes Active Directory (and if you have more than twenty-five users, there is a decent chance that you do), you can integrate Active Directory with Office 365 and manage your user accounts from Active Directory.

That feature is probably only exciting to the firm's IT person, but there's also something that users will like: **Single-Sign On**, so they won't have to enter their username and password twice to sign into the local network and Office 365.

The Midsize Business plan is a little different in the pricing and contract area as well. First, the pricing is $15 per mailbox per month and unlike Small Business Premium there's no discount for paying the whole year up front. Sec-

> Active Directory is how a Microsoft Windows domain keeps track of its users. That's where you create and manage user accounts.

ondly unlike Small Business, to which you can subscribe to on a month-to-month basis, the Midsize Business plan has an annual commitment. Although you can cancel the plan at any time, you may have to pay a penalty for early termination.

Like the Small Business Premium plan, the Midsize Business plan has a thirty-day free trial if you'd like to try before you buy.

Enterprise E1

Like the idea of Office 365 Small Business but have twenty-six or more users? Then Enterprise E1 might be your answer. It has basically the same features of Small Business—50GB Exchange Mailboxes, 25GB of OneDrive for Business storage per user, 10GB (plus 500MB per user) of SharePoint space and Lync. But since it's a member of the Enterprise family, it's available to an unlimited number of mailboxes.

Also like the Small Business plan, Enterprise E1 does *not* include the locally installed Microsoft Office applications, so if you're happy with your current version of Office, you can keep it. Really. However, if you have a version of Outlook older than Outlook 2007, you won't be using it to access your 50GB Exchange mailbox. Sorry.

Like the Midsize Business plan, the E1 plan includes Active Directory integration for management and single sign-on.

The Enterprise plans like E1 do add one other new trick though— Yammer Enterprise is included. We'll talk more about Yammer in Chapter 5, but basically it's Microsoft's new enterprise-class social networking tool. You can have collaborative discussions and share files and notes within the private environment of Yammer.

The E1 plan is priced at $8 per mailbox per month, and like the midsize plan, it has an annual commitment and no discount for pre-paying for the year.

Enterprise E3

The next plan up is the E3 plan, which is the Enterprise analog to the Small Business Premium plan. E3 includes 50GB Exchange mailboxes, 25GB of OneDrive for Business Cloud storage for each user, 10GB (plus 500MB per user) of SharePoint, plus Lync. With the E3 plan, you also get the full local install of Microsoft Office and the Active Directory integration.

What makes the E3 plan different (and possibly worth the price tag) is that it adds advanced e-mail capabilities such as **Information Rights Management**, encryption, **unlimited online archiving**, and **legal hold** capabilities. Additionally, you get an **eDiscovery Center** that supports search across Exchange mailboxes and SharePoint team sites.

Wait, what happened to E2?

There originally was an E2 plan that sat between E1 and E3 but Microsoft decided it didn't make sense to keep it so they rolled its features into the E1 plan and just did away with E2.

The eDiscovery Center supports **In-Place Hold**, which preserves data in the event of litigation that may require it to be produced. One of the interesting features of In-Place Hold is that it lets your users continue to work with, and even edit, the content while preserving the original versions unmodified behind the scenes, so they can be produced if necessary.

The eDiscovery Center also lets you do a **Search and Export** across the organization (or at least that portion of the organization that is hosted in Office 365) for key words or phrases. Let me reiterate the significance that it will do it across the *entire* organization. No more searching individual mailboxes for relevant items; the eDiscovery Center will search across all of them.

Finally, the version of Lync that comes with the E3 plan adds hosted voicemail support with auto-attendant capabilities, so if you want to press 4...you can.

What's the price tag for all of that you may be wondering? It's $20 per mailbox per month on an annual commitment.

Is there an E4?

Yes, there is, though the primary capability that E4 adds to the equation is the ability to use Lync as a VOIP phone system. We'll touch on that briefly in Chapter 6, though I have yet to see many firms choosing to pay the $22 per mailbox per month, plus deploying an on-premises Lync server as well.

Office 365 Pro Plus

Most of the firms we work with want to have at least Microsoft Exchange, but occasionally we meet a firm that only wants to have the latest version of Microsoft Office without all of the other services. For those folks, there's Office 365 Pro Plus. Pro Plus gives you the full, locally installed Office suite that you can install on up to five PCs or Macs. Also, you get licenses for Office Mobile that lets you have things like Excel for iPad.

Among the plans we've talked about in this chapter, Pro Plus is actually unique in that it is actually licensed per *user* rather than per mailbox—good thing because Pro Plus doesn't include any mailboxes.

Office 365 Pro Plus is $12 per month per *user*, which you might recognize as being only 50 cents per month cheaper than Office 365 Small Business Premium. If you have fewer than twenty-five users, it's probably worth it to spend the extra 50 cents per month to get the full suite with Exchange, SharePoint, and Lync. For larger firms, the math is a little trickier since they'd likely be looking at the $15 per month Midsize package or the $20 per month E3 offering.

Working with a Partner of Record

You're not required to work with a Microsoft Partner—what is known internally as a partner of record—to get and deploy Office 365, but there are a few good reasons why you might want to. Full disclosure as we start this topic, my firm—Roland Schorr & Tower—are Microsoft Partners ourselves.

First, the Microsoft Partner can bring a lot of field expertise to the migration. Chances are, even if you have in-house IT, they haven't done many Office 365 migrations or deployments. While they can probably figure it out, it's usually nice to have an experienced partner to assist—especially considering that we're talking about some of the most mission-critical systems in your firm.

Second, the partner may be more responsive than Microsoft. All of the business-class Office 365 plans include 24x7 phone support, but reviews of that support are often mixed. Plus, if you call Microsoft support, you're getting somebody who may be an expert on Office 365 but probably doesn't know anything about your firm or your environment. Working with a partner, you'll more often get somebody who is familiar with how your firm operates.

Third, if you have a partner of record listed on your account, it indicates to Microsoft that you're already working with a partner. That means you're less likely to get spammed with offers trying to upsell you. Also, your partner of record may have some advantages when it comes to calling Microsoft on your behalf for support or account issues.

Fourth, if your partner has delegated administration rights (our next topic, be patient) that means the partner can help you administer your account, create or delete users, reset passwords, and make other tweaks for you.

Buying Office 365 through a Microsoft Partner does not have to change your pricing structure or whom you pay. Our clients pay Microsoft the exact same $4, $6, $12.50, or whatever per mailbox per month that they would otherwise. Our clients only pay us when we actually provide them with services.

Do you have to use a partner of record? No, but there's very little downside to it, and there can be some nice advantages. You can even add a partner of record to your account long after you've already started using Office 365 if you want to gain that level of support. It doesn't cost anything to add the partner to an existing account either.

How Do I Find an Office 365 Partner?

Obviously I'd like it if you called us, but if you'd prefer to find a different partner to work with, you can find one at http://office365. pinpoint.microsoft.com or ask around to find other firms who are already running Office 365 and see if they have a partner they liked working with.

Delegated Administration

If you're working with a Microsoft Partner, you should give the partner **delegated administration rights**. With delegated administration, your partner has a control panel that they can use to assist you in administering your account (see Figure 2.5). Can a partner do things you can't do? No, but a partner can probably do them faster and with fewer errors simply because a good partner does these things all the time.

Figure 2.5   The Delegated Administration Control Panel

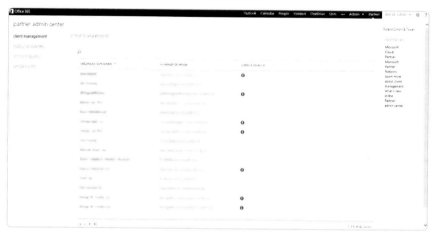

We've had clients call us and ask us to add users for them, change user names, add e-mail aliases, distribution lists, external contacts…all sorts of tasks that we can do with just a few mouse clicks but that might take the client quite a while to figure out. One firm administrator called us from the beach where she was on vacation to ask us to reset her senior partner's password. He'd forgotten it, and she didn't want to cut her beach day short to go back to the hotel room, fire up the laptop and reset it herself.

There's no cost to granting your partner delegated administration rights, and you can revoke those rights from the Office 365 portal if you ever want to.

What You Need to Know

It's important to understand that Office 365 is usually priced by the mailbox rather than by the user or device. There are a number of different SKUs (versions) of Office 365 and the one that is right for your firm depends upon how many mailboxes you have (or want) and what mix of software and services you want. The subscription model may make you a bit uneasy at first, but that's the way the software business is moving. Soon most major pieces of software will be sold that way.

There are three families of Office 365 software—Small Business, Midsize, and Enterprise. You can mix-and-match licenses within the families—for example twenty seats of E1 and fifteen seats of E3—but you can't easily mix and match licenses across families. Also, while it's now easy to move up to a bigger family (from Small Business to Midsize, for example), it's not easy to go the other way.

A number of good Microsoft Partners are available for you to work with. Though you don't have to have a partner to get Office 365, the benefits of working with a knowledgeable partner can be more than worth the modest costs. If you do decide to work with a partner, consider giving the partner delegated administration rights to your Office 365 subscription so the partner can give you better assistance when you need it.

Next up—let's take a look at Microsoft Office.

Chapter 3

Microsoft Office

Office 365 is rapidly becoming the preferred way to get the latest version of Microsoft Office. As of this writing, it's called **Microsoft Office 2013**, but the odds are good that in the next year or so Microsoft will drop the year designation and simply call it Microsoft Office.

In addition, Microsoft's Click-to-Run delivery system is rapidly becoming the way the company wants to deliver software. The

If you had any experience with Click-to-Run in Office 2010, you might be cringing right now. Back then, Click-to-Run was often challenging and frequently didn't work at all with add-ins like document management systems. Microsoft heard that feedback, though, and they completely redesigned it for Office 2013. The new Click-to-Run is much better than the old one, and compatibility problems are few.

days of buying a box with a DVD in it and installing from that DVD are fading. If you buy Microsoft Office from Office 365, it will install by streaming to your machine over the Internet.

To be clear, the Click-to-Run software *is* locally installed on your machine. Though you do need an Internet connection to install it, you don't need an Internet connection to run it.

But I Like My Version of Microsoft Office, Do I **Have** to Upgrade It?

Not necessarily, but it depends upon your version of Office. Office 2003 and earlier are no longer supported, so you will have to upgrade those if you want to use Office with the Office 365 services. And frankly, since they're no longer supported, you really *should* upgrade them even if you're not going to use Office 365 services. That said, if you have Office 2007, then you will probably *want* to upgrade it. Office 2013 has some new features that Office 2007 doesn't have. If you have Office 2010, the decision is somewhat more difficult.

Let's take a few minutes to take a look at what each of the products in the Microsoft Office suite are and what you can do with them.

Outlook

Most people think of Outlook as just an e-mail program, but actually Outlook is Microsoft's **personal information manager** too. About 20 years ago, Microsoft Outlook evolved out of the merger of two products called **Microsoft Exchange Client** and **Schedule+**. As you might imagine, that means being a client to Microsoft Exchange server (see Chapter 4) runs deep in its digital DNA.

What's New in Outlook 2013?

1. **Improved Editor.** The changes and improvements to Microsoft Word appear in Outlook too. That means Word's smoother editing, screenshots, and online pictures are available for your e-mails as well.

2. **Inline Reply Editor.** Want to reply to a message you're reading in the Reading Pane? Now you can reply *in* the reading pane. It's a nifty time saver you have to experience to really appreciate.

3. **Peeks.** The To Do Bar is gone, but you can now get some of that functionality in a modular fashion. If you hover your mouse over one of the modules along the bottom of the window, a little preview pops up that shows you some of the content from that module (like your next few appointments in the Calendar) and gives you the ability to do a search or add a new item.

4. **Weather.** Go to the Calendar module and you'll notice that just above the Calendar in most of the views, you'll see a three-day weather forecast for whatever ZIP codes you specify.

5. **People Cards.** These are one of the biggest changes in the new Outlook. People cards are what you'll see if you search for a person using the **Search People** field on the **Ribbon** or with the **People view** selected in the **People folder** (formerly **Contacts**).

6. **More flexibility in the Folder Pane.** Folders don't have to be in alphabetical order anymore—now you can sort them however you want...and resort them in alpha order with one click too.

There are a lot more new features, like improved security and anti-phishing capabilities, postmarks, Free/Busy information management, 32- and 64-bit versions, and a lot of other subtle things that will really excite your consultant or IT person but that might be a tad esoteric for you. I'll mention them throughout the book, but mostly I want to focus on the features and tools that you're really going to use and care about in your daily practice. If you really embrace Outlook as a personal information manager—and not just an e-mail client—you'll realize the true power of the product.

With Outlook 2013, you can connect not only to multiple Exchange mailboxes but also to multiple Exchange servers if you need to. When you first start Outlook 2013, you might wonder what's become of the **To Do Bar** that Outlook 2010 users have become so dependent upon. With Outlook 2013, you "roll your own" so to speak by going to the **View** tab of the **Ribbon** and adding the modules (**Tasks**, **Calendar**, **People**) that you want to appear on the To Do Bar, and you can specify the order in which they appear.

Want to learn more about Microsoft Outlook 2013? Look for the Law Practice Division's book *The Lawyer's Guide to Microsoft Outlook 2013* written by…well…me!

Let's take a quick tour of Outlook 2013's other capabilities.

E-mail

Most people are familiar with Outlook's e-mail feature, and as part of the Office 365 suite, it's more powerful than ever. Too many attorneys are still using antiquated POP3 or IMAP e-mail protocols for their messages. There are a number of problems with that in modern practice:

- POP3 was never designed for multiple devices. It downloads your Inbox (and only your Inbox) but actual synchronization is non-existent.

- IMAP does a better job of synchronization, and multiple folders, but it's clunky and unreliable, and it doesn't synchronize calendars, contacts, or tasks.
- Most POP3 or IMAP mailboxes, especially from small Internet providers, have small mailbox quotas not well-suited to attorneys who tend to be pack-rats when it comes to e-mail.
- Both POP3 and IMAP tend to synchronize on a schedule. It's not recommended that you have Outlook poll your POP3 mailbox, for example, more often than every five to ten minutes. Though in reality that's often enough, many users are too impatient for that schedule.

Caution: Geek Content Ahead!

POP3 stands for Post Office Protocol version 3. **IMAP** stands for Internet Message Access Protocol. MAPI (we're getting to it) is, rather remarkably, an improvement over "Messaging Application Program Interface" which is a protocol Microsoft uses to transmit data between Exchange Server and MAPI-compatible clients like Outlook. RPC is Remote Procedure Call, which is another protocol Exchange server uses (often in conjunction with MAPI) to connect with clients.

Outlook, when paired with Exchange Server, as it almost always is in Office 365, uses the Exchange protocols of MAPI and RPC. These protocols provide for very robust synchronization of the entire mailbox, including subfolders, calendars, contacts, and tasks. Better still, **Exchange ActiveSync** connects to almost every kind of portable device: smartphones, tablets, and more so that you can keep your mailbox in perfect sync whether you're in or out of the office.

There's a reason Outlook is the preferred e-mail client of nearly all of the Fortune 500 and nearly all of the AmLaw 100: it's powerful. With Outlook, you can file your e-mail into subfolders simply by dragging and dropping the messages or by pressing **CTRL+-SHIFT+V** on your keyboard. You can also create rules (using the **Rules Wizard**) that automatically manage incoming messages.

You can create e-mails that are not only text but also include embedded images, tables, and figures. You can insert attachments. When you receive certain kinds of attachments (such as Word, PowerPoint, Excel, and Acrobat), you can read those attachments without ever opening them, simply by clicking the attachment in the message header and reading the attachment in the reading pane.

In Outlook 2013, you can also use the reading pane to reply to messages. Simply click the Reply, Reply to All or Forward buttons at the top of the reading pane and Outlook will let you edit and send your reply right there in the reading pane without ever having to open a new window.

Outlook also lets you create **contact groups**—pre-made groups of contacts that you want to send the same e-mails to. Addressing your e-mail message to the contact group saves time over adding each of the recipients individually.

Another new feature for Outlook 2013's e-mail capability is the ability to manually re-sort folders. In past versions, the folders only sorted alphabetically. With 2013, you can manually drag the folders up or down in the list as you like.

Calendar

Another Outlook feature that is important to attorneys is the Calendar. Outlook's calendar does all of the things you'd expect a calendar to do—you can schedule meetings, appointments and events, include start and end times, and even enter locations and notes.

If you have a smartphone, be sure to use the location field for any appointment outside the office—when most smartphones synchronize your calendar, they will turn the location field into a clickable link that will launch your GPS Navigation app and give you turn-by-turn directions to your destination (often with traffic reports).

Some of the more advanced features of the Calendar, however, are what really appeal to lawyers. First of all, you can easily color-code your calendar by using **Categories** to apply different colors to different kinds of appointments. Trials might be red. Meetings with prospective clients perhaps green. Meetings with committees within your firm could be blue. Whatever the color scheme you select, it's easy to tell at a glance what your day looks like.

Another feature of Outlook, in conjunction with Office 365's Exchange server, is the ability to share calendars. This is a big one with attorneys who like to share their calendar with an assistant who can manage their calendar for them. With Outlook and Exchange, it's easy to share your calendar with others in your firm—giving them the level of permissions and access that's appropriate. With the calendar that you want to share selected, go to the **Folder** tab of the **Ribbon** and select **Share Calendar.** Outlook will let you select whom to share it with and whether that person (or those persons) should be allowed to add or edit items or only be able to read them.

Contacts—AKA People

The Contacts feature of Outlook has always been very popular, and with Outlook 2013 this has been renamed **People** and has a new, and somewhat controversial, look to it (see Figure 3.1).

Figure 3.1   The People Pane

With People, you can keep a database of your contacts, along with key contact information like e-mail address, phone numbers, mailing addresses and notes about the person. Outlook's contact card can actually store up to nineteen phone numbers for each contact, even though the contact page where you enter that information only shows four phone numbers at once. Click the drop-down arrow next to each phone number label to choose a different phone number to display.

Likewise, the addresses field can store up to three different addresses, though it only displays one at a time. Below the button that indicates which address you're looking at is a checkbox for **This is the mailing address**. That's a deceptively useful checkbox; if you have contacts who have a street address and a P.O. Box, for example, you might enter their street address as their business address and their P.O. Box as their Other address. By checking the **Mailing Address** checkbox while the **Other** is displayed, Outlook will know that when you do a mail merge and select Mailing Address as the address to use, for that client, the P.O. Box is the desired destination.

If the new People view bothers you, it's easy to revert to the old view by clicking **View** then **Change View** on the **Ribbon** and selecting the old **Business Card** view.

Tasks

Outlook has a very capable Tasks feature, though not as many people use it as you might expect. In Outlook 2003, Microsoft realized that not as many users were using the Tasks feature as they expected and they surmised this was because *out of sight* means "out of mind," and users spent most of their time in the **Inbox** where they couldn't see their tasks list. The solution was the **To Do Bar**, which in earlier versions of Outlook appeared along the right side of the screen, even when you were in the Inbox.

When you first start Office 2013, you may be a little shocked to discover that the To Do Bar no longer appears by default. In fact, you have to assemble it yourself. Click on the **View** tab of the **Ribbon** and click **To Do Bar**. Select the elements (**Calendar**, **People**, **Tasks**) you'd like to appear on your To Do Bar, but take care in the order you select them. The first item you select will be at the top of the To Do Bar, the second item you select will be below that, and if you select the third item, that will appear at the bottom.

To create new tasks, you can click the **New Items** button at the top of the **Inbox** and select **Task** to open the **Task inspector** (see Figure 3.3). From there just give your task a title and, preferably, a due date. The rest of the fields are optional. You can also quickly create a task right from the **To Do Bar** by typing the title of your task in the **Type a new task** field that appears by default at the top of the tasks list.

Figure 3.2   The Task Inspector

When your task is complete, you can just click the **flag icon** on the **To Do Bar** to mark it complete, or you can right-click the task and click **Mark Complete**.

Word

Word is one of the most venerable, and most often used, programs in the Microsoft Office suite. I probably don't have to tell you what it does because for most of you, it's the tool that you use to get your work done every day.

That said, I'll take this space to highlight some of the changes in recent versions that are relevant to attorneys, so you can make an informed decision about upgrading.

Word 2013 places a fairly strong emphasis on improving the look and layout of your documents. The **Design** tab offers a number of easily applied themes, formats, and colors that you can set for your document. Another new feature are the **Alignment Guides**, which can help you line your text up properly, especially when you have objects like images or tables on the page.

In Word 2010, the **Reading Mode** that Word defaulted to when you opened a Word document from an attachment wasn't universally beloved. It's been improved in 2013, so that it resizes the document better and lets you flip through the pages more easily. The experience feels more like reading a book on a Kindle or other e-reader than the old version did. If the new version still doesn't appeal to you, you can still turn it off in **Word > Options**.

Want to learn more about Microsoft Word 2013? Look for the Law Practice Division's book *The Lawyer's Guide to Microsoft Word 2013* written by guess who? Yes, me again!

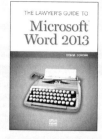

THE LAWYER'S GUIDE TO
Microsoft
Word 2013

When you're creating your text in Word 2013, a very subtle change has been made to the way the cursor moves across the screen. It's been animated very subtlety to move more smoothly as you type. It sounds like a little thing...but it's really quite nice.

Another improvement in Word 2013 is the **threaded comments** (see Figure 3.3). In the past, if somebody added a comment to a Word document, you could add a separate comment right after that. Then that person would post another separate comment replying to you, and...it could get messy really quickly. Word 2013 has threaded comments, so you can post a reply to someone's comment that goes right there in his or her comment. And the other person can reply and then you can reply...and it all stays together as a single comment string.

Figure 3.3 Threaded Comments Make It Easy to Follow the Discussion

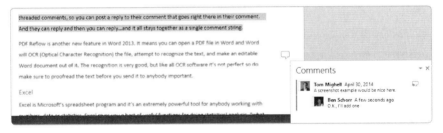

PDF Reflow is another new feature in Word 2013. It means you can open a PDF file in Word, and Word will use **OCR** (Optical Character Recognition) technology to analyze the file, attempt to recognize the text, and make an editable Word document out of it. The recognition is very good, but like all OCR software it's not perfect, so do make sure to proofread the text before you send it to anybody important.

Do you need to upgrade Word? Not necessarily—but as I said at the beginning of Chapter 2: if you're using Word 2003, yes, you should upgrade it. If you're using Word 2007 you may want to upgrade. If you're using Word 2010 then you might not want to bother.

Excel

Excel is Microsoft's spreadsheet program, and it's an extremely powerful tool for anybody working with numbers, data, or statistics. Excel gives you a host of useful functions for doing statistical analysis, "what-if" scenarios, and analyzing data. Lawyers can use Excel to work through complicated financial or settlement scenarios and see how changes to one or more elements affect the bottom line. You can easily create charts and graphs to present your data as well.

Excel 2013 has some new capabilities to make you smile. One of the most dramatic is **Flash Fill**, which does predictive data entry. That means that Excel will try to recognize patterns in the data you're entering (formats or values), and it suggests the data it thinks you're going to enter. It's not perfect, but it's very good. That can save you a *lot* of time. You can also use Flash Fill to extract content from a set of cells, such as extracting just the month from a date or extracting just the first name from a cell containing the full name.

Excel 2013 has some new tools for helping you to analyze your data as well. The new **Quick Analysis** tool can offer suggestions for the best ways to analyze a selected set of data, so that you can better make sense of it.

One feature most Excel users have heard of but few have actually used are **Pivot Tables**. Pivot Tables allow you to take a table of information and look at in different ways. For example, perhaps you have a table showing

Want to learn more about Microsoft Excel 2013? Look for the Law Practice Division's book *The Lawyer's Guide to Microsoft Excel 2013* written by...OK, yes, this is another one of mine.

THE LAWYER'S GUIDE TO
Microsoft
Excel 2013

sales across multiple states across multiple years. A Pivot Table can let you arrange that so that you can see sales by state in a particular year, or sales in a particular year across all of the states. In Excel 2013, Microsoft has made it easier to create and customize Pivot Tables, so you can look at your data in whole new ways.

PowerPoint

PowerPoint is Microsoft's presentation program. It's taken a lot of ribbing over the years because it's the most widely used presentation program. Because it's so widely used, it's often badly used. In PowerPoint, you create a set of pages or slides,

Want to learn more about Microsoft PowerPoint? Look for the Law Practice Division's book *PowerPoint in One Hour for Lawyers* written by...did you guess me? Well, if so you're wrong...this one is by Paul Unger.

known collectively as a **slide deck**, which you then page through one by one to accompany your presentation. If you've attended a conference or CLE in the last two decades, you've undoubtedly seen PowerPoint in action.

To be honest, PowerPoint 2013 is not, for what most lawyers do, significantly different from PowerPoint 2010. It's got a slightly slicker interface, and **Presentation View** (where the audience sees the slides on the big screen and you see a nifty presentation management console on your smaller screen) has been improved (see Figure 3.4). Otherwise, PowerPoint is fundamentally the same.

Figure 3.4   PowerPoint Presentation View

OneNote

OneNote is Microsoft's free-form note-taking, collaboration, and research tool. OneNote uses the metaphor of a spiral-bound notebook, divided into tabbed sections, and within each section is a collection of pages. Because OneNote is digital, a notebook can have an almost unlimited number of sections, and each section can have a nearly unlimited number of pages. Of course, you can also have many, many notebooks. The real power comes from OneNote's ability to search across those many notebooks, sections, and pages to locate words or phrases you may have typed...or even inked.

> Want to learn more about Microsoft OneNote? Look for the Law Practice Division's book *OneNote in One Hour for Lawyers* written by...OK, yes, this one is another one of mine. I really need a hobby.

OneNote also lets you insert other content. You can drag and drop content from web pages. You can record and embed audio or video notes. You can insert images from a camera, scanner, or file.

And you can even share those notes quite effectively with colleagues. If they have OneNote as well (and they certainly could, as Microsoft recently made it available for free)—they can view and edit the notes, and their edits will appear on your notebook often within moments of making the edits.

OneNote then is a powerful tool for gathering ideas, information, and content and collaborating on that content with your team.

Publisher

Too many attorneys use Word to do desktop publishing—for creating flyers, cards, brochures, and other graphical material—but in reality, Publisher is the tool that's best suited for that task. With previous versions of the Microsoft Office suite, if you had the Home and Business version of the suite, you didn't get Publisher. With Office 365, Publisher 2013 is included. Publisher makes it easier to insert and work with images, and it offers a host of new picture and text effects to make your designs more appealing.

Publisher offers a wide variety of pre-made templates to get you started on your flyers, brochures, certificates, or whatever you need (see Figure 3.5), *and* you can customize them. Publisher also makes it easy to provide an electronic file to a professional print shop, so the staff can produce boxes and boxes of your graphical creation.

Figure 3.5   Publisher Offers Many Useful Templates

Access

Databases are all around us—many systems are in actuality just databases—and Access is Microsoft's database tool. It's true that *some* database tasks can be done by Excel, but if you're talking about a database with thousands (and especially with tens or hundreds of thousands) of records, Microsoft Access is far more powerful.

Microsoft has done a *lot* of work to make creating useful databases in Microsoft Access easier for average folks. As a result, there are a number of templates and pre-created database designs that you can choose from, as you see in Figure 3.6. You can start from one of those designs, and then customize that database as you see fit to suit your own needs.

Figure 3.6 Access Offers Pre-created Database Designs

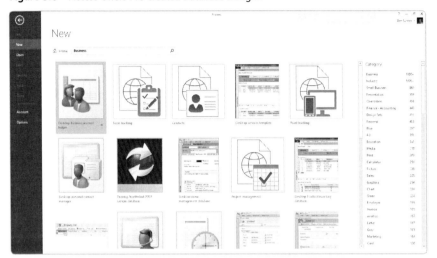

Access is a **relational database**, which means that rather than having a single table that contains all of the records, you can have multiple tables that are linked together via some common key field. That lets you more efficiently store and manage large sets of data.

Access 2013 is one of the few products in the 2013 suite that has actually been significantly depreciated however. If your intent is to create powerful and robust local database projects, you might actually be happier with Access 2010. In Access 2013, the focus has shifted from creating those local databases to creating database web parts for SharePoint sites. That's cool and powerful, but it might not be exactly what you wanted. Can you still create local databases with Access 2013? Sure. But it's not what Access 2013 is primarily about.

InfoPath

Of course, nothing could be more depreciated than Microsoft InfoPath—which is already on its way to vanishing. Microsoft has already announced that InfoPath will be going away soon and is likely to be replaced by an as-yet unannounced product. InfoPath is a tool for creating electronic forms that your users, or your clients, can fill out and submit electronically.

For those who might get a chance to play with InfoPath in its final incarnation, you should know that InfoPath is actually two programs, not one.

InfoPath Designer

With InfoPath Designer you can create elaborate XML forms that you can distribute. The forms can have a variety of useful controls on them such as date pickers, radio buttons, spin wheels, and more. Some firms have used these forms to publish client intake forms that prospective clients can complete and submit to the firm for review and consideration. The forms can be published to a website or used locally with the companion product. Which brings us to…

InfoPath Filler

InfoPath Filler is the companion application that is sometimes used to fill out forms that were created in InfoPath Designer. Filler doesn't let the user change or modify the form, other than to supply and submit the requested information.

It will be interesting to see what Microsoft replaces Info-Path with.

Project

Microsoft Project is one of the more powerful, and least-used client applications that Microsoft offers. Traditionally, the knock on Project has been that unless the project you're doing is fairly substantial, it can take longer to set it up than to actually do the project. The fact is, though, many major companies use Microsoft Project to manage their big projects...and for a law firm, your projects are your matters. We've started to see interest from firms in using Project as a matter management system for large cases.

Additionally, with Project, you can set up templates for the various kinds of matters you handle, which can dramatically reduce the set-up time. You could have a standard template for a probate matter, for example, that you simply customize a bit to reflect the details of a particular case.

Microsoft Project is not included with any of the standard SKUs of Microsoft Office 365. There is a separate SKU called Project Pro for Office 365 that is available for $25 per user per month.

With Project you start by defining your firm's working parameters—you enter the hours of the day and days of the week that you work. Project uses this information to create the timelines —if you have a matter that you estimate will take thirty hours of work you don't want Project to estimate that will finish in 1.5 days, unless you just don't bother sleeping. You can also enter days or weeks when you want to limit the amount of time available to a project—due to holidays, other cases, or any other interruptions you foresee.

With the calendar sorted, you can add resources to your matter: associates, paralegals, experts...even non-human resources like conference rooms or special equipment. You can even assign a cost to each of those resources so you can get a good estimate of what this matter is going to cost you—which can be very helpful in evaluating pricing to your client.

Finally into that matrix of time and resources you enter your tasks: interviewing witnesses, document review, preparing briefs, and events like trial setting conferences, and so on. Some tasks may run concurrently (such as different kinds of discovery that may happen at more or less the same time), while others may be dependent on completing previous tasks. For example, ninety days after a certain document is filed, you may have a mandatory conference. Project can sort all of that out for you.

Microsoft Project will prepare a **Gantt Chart** (see Figure 3.7) for you that estimates the start and finish date as well as the dates of expected milestones. By assigning your resources to the various tasks, Project can make sure you're not over-utilizing anybody (assigning the same associate to do document review *and* attend out-of-town depositions on the same matter on the same day, for example) as well as prepare a total cost estimate for the matter.

Figure 3.7   The Timeline of the Matter

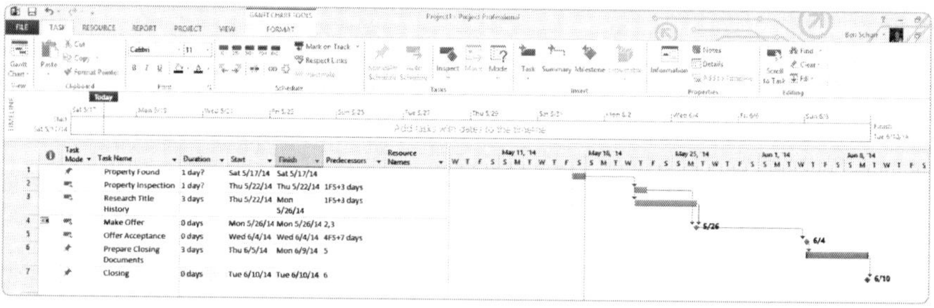

As you proceed through the matter, you can enter the actual time spent on each task, and Project can map that against your expected time to let you know if you're ahead of or behind schedule and whether you're still on budget. By showing you the specific tasks that are running ahead or behind, Project can help you manage things to get the matter back on track.

Finally, Project can produce a number of detailed reports to help you evaluate the matter—which can be extremely helpful in improving your processes and your billing on future matters of this type.

Once you have a well-defined and curated Project created for a particular type of matter, you should save that matter as a template to use as a starting point for all future

> By creating **Resource Pools**, Microsoft Project can check a resource's schedule across multiple matters. That way you won't accidentally schedule an associate for twenty-five hours in the same day across different matters.

matters of that type. Once you have that template, you should only need to adjust the Start Date for each future matter and tweak a few of the particulars—and you can quickly have a project plan in place for the new matter.

Particularly for lengthy or complex matters and where alternative billing arrangements like flat fees are involved, Microsoft Project can be a powerful tool for managing your team and making sure you're as efficient and effective as possible.

Installing Office 2013

To install Office 2013 from Office 365 you need three things:

1. **A SKU of Office 365 That Actually Includes Office 2013.** Office 365 Small Business does not. Office 365 Small Business Premium does. Office 365 Midsize does. Office 365 E1 does not. See the "Does Your Plan Include Office?" box in Chapter 2 for the full comparison

2. **An Internet Connection.** Office 2013 installs via a stream from the web. If you don't have an especially fast Internet connection and your computer is portable, you might consider going somewhere that does have a fast connection.

To your house, a friend's house, Internet Café…somewhere. Over a slow connection, the Office 2013 install can take a while.

3. **A Web Browser.** Logging in and starting the process of installing Office 365 happens via the web.

To install Office 2013 on your machine, once those prerequisites are met do this:

1. Log into your Office 365 portal (http://portal.office365.com) with your e-mail address and Office 365 password.

2. Click the **Settings** button (which looks like a gear) at the top right corner (see Figure 3.8).

Figure 3.8   The Settings Button

3. Click **Office 365 Settings > Software**

4. On the software page (see Figure 3.9), you'll find **Install the latest version of Office**. Click the **Install** button under that and Office will begin to stream to your computer. Over a fast connection, this can take a few minutes. Over a slow connection, I've seen it take the better part of an hour.

Figure 3.9   The Software Page

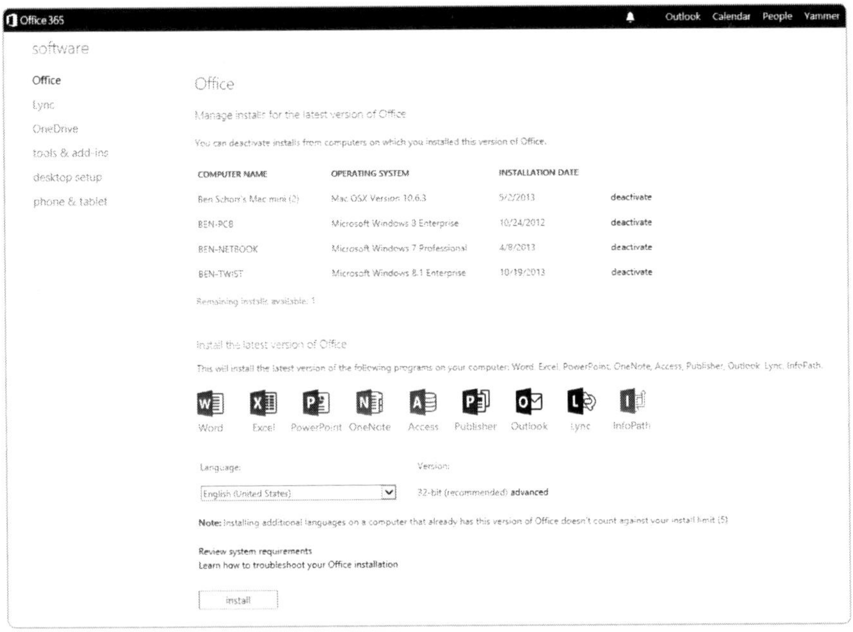

For Mobile Devices

Microsoft has been making a big push lately to get its applications onto as many mobile platforms as possible. It would be futile to give you too many details in this book since the mobile apps iterate even faster than the desktop ones do. That said, I can certainly introduce them. You can find the mobile apps for all of the platforms by going to the Office 365 portal (http://portal.office365.com) and clicking the **Settings** button at the top right corner and selecting **Office 365 Settings**. On the page that appears, select **Software** and then **Phone & Tablet**.

Windows Phone

One of the first questions I get is "How good is Word on a Windows Phone?" Well, I'm writing this paragraph on my Nokia

Lumia 928. It's not bad. I wouldn't want to write the entire book this way, but for quick edits, it's fine.

I can't give you any instructions for installing Office on a Windows Phone because...well, there aren't any. Office comes preinstalled on Windows Phone 8. Nothing you need to do; it's already there. Just click on the **Apps** page and select **Office** to start it. You'll find Word, Excel, and PowerPoint there. OneNote is also installed on Windows Phone, but it appears as a separate app.

Lync is available for Windows Phone as a free download in the store.

Android

You can find the Android version of Office Mobile in the **Play Store**, but it's probably easier to log into your Office 365 web portal, click **Settings** > **Office 365 Settings** > **Software** and on the left side navigation pane select **Phone & Tablet**. One of the options there is **Android** and you can simply click the **Get App** button to have the app sent wirelessly to your device.

Office Mobile, OneNote, and Lync are all available for Android.

iPhone

For iPhone, the story is basically the same as for Android. Though you may find most of the Office apps in the **iTunes Store**, it's usually easier to get them from the Office 365 portal. Go to the same software page that I described for Android, select **iPhone** as your device and **Get Apps** to get Office Mobile, OneNote, **OWA**, Lync, and SharePoint apps.

To be fair, the OWA app is really just a browser interface to Outlook Web Access. Most of our clients choose to use **Exchange ActiveSync** integration in the default iPhone mail, calendar and contacts apps to get to their Exchange mailboxes.

iPad

The newest member of the Office 365 client family is the iPad. As with the Android and iPhone, you can find the apps for this under the Software page of Office 365 Settings. For the iPad, you can download Word, Excel, PowerPoint, OneNote, OWA, Lync, and SharePoint. Just as with the iPhone, most of our clients skip the OWA app and just use the iPad's own e-mail, calendar, and contacts apps.

What You Need to Know

Office 2013 is the newest iteration of the Microsoft Office suite. It's more evolutionary than revolutionary, but most of the products in the suite did get at least a few useful enhancements. As we discussed in Chapter 2, not all of the Office 365 packages include Office 2013, but of the ones that do it is the full, local, install of Microsoft Office—much like what you're accustomed to.

Microsoft is increasingly getting on board with the movement to mobile, and that means there are now mobile versions of the main Office products; Word, Excel, PowerPoint, and OneNote, especially for all of the major mobile platforms.

Chapter 4

Exchange Server

When it comes to e-mail, calendar, and contacts, no system is more widely deployed in the Fortune 500 or the AmLaw 100 than Microsoft's Exchange Server. It's a powerful, scalable, full-featured, and reliable system for business e-mail. Traditionally, you would have to do as the AmLaw 100 firms did—deploy your own, on-premise Microsoft Exchange server. Unfortunately that set-up also came with an AmLaw 100 kind of price tag. Now, thanks to Office 365, solo, small, and midsized firms can afford all of the Exchange Server functionality for an extremely reasonable monthly fee.

Introduction to Microsoft Exchange

Microsoft Exchange Server made its debut back in 1995 when it was curiously named **Exchange Server 4.0** even though the public had never seen Exchange Servers 1–3. Exchange was an evolution for the **Microsoft Mail** product Microsoft had before.

At its most basic, Exchange Server is a database that contains e-mail boxes.

Microsoft quickly realized, however, that the product could be much more than that. If you're sending and receiving e-mail from people, you also want to have a contacts list of people you connect with often, and as long as you have that contacts list, it's trivial to add fields for phone numbers, postal addresses, company name, and more. Taking the next logical step, Microsoft realized that business people also needed to be able to track their schedule, so a calendar feature was added.

In 2000, Microsoft switched the naming of Exchange Server from version numbers to years and today the state of the art version of Microsoft Exchange Server is **Exchange Server 2013**. Exchange 2013 has come a *long* way from the version that debuted nearly two decades before. Today's features include:

- **Exchange ActiveSync.** A protocol that allows smartphones, tablets, and other devices to get mail, calendar, contacts, and tasks pushed to them from an Exchange server on an almost real-time basis

- **Outlook Web Access.** A web-based client that allows a user to view his or her entire mailbox, including folders, calendar, contacts, and tasks from within a web browser on any Internet-connected computer. Outlook Web Access, which is frequently referred to as OWA, has evolved over the years to more closely match the look and functionality of the desktop Outlook client we talked about in Chapter 3. You can even right-click on items in the OWA environment and get a context menu!

- **Dramatically Faster Search.** Improved indexing and searching across mailboxes

Exchange maintains a central list of mailboxes (and groups and contacts, which we'll talk about later), which is referred to as the **Global Address List**. The most important (and common) part of the global address list are mailboxes.

Mailboxes

The central concept you need to understand about Office 365's Exchange Server is that it's all about mailboxes. The mailbox contains the user's e-mail and all of the e-mail folders, but it also contains the calendar, contacts, tasks and other folders (such as Notes or Journal). As of this writing, all Office 365 Exchange mailboxes, except for the **Kiosk/K1** plans, have at least 50GB of capacity. That's quite large.

> The Kiosk/K1 plans are inexpensive Office 365 plans that are intended for users who don't actually have their own computers. It's hard to think of many scenarios in a law firm where that might apply—perhaps in-house messengers or mailroom staff who don't have a PC—but in industry, it's sometimes used for warehouse workers, drivers, delivery folks, and others who might not have access to their own computer. The Kiosk plans are quite limited—basically they're just intended to provide those users with a small mailbox where they can receive company announcements and such.

A single-user account has just one mailbox associated with it, though it is possible (but not that common) in Outlook for a person to open multiple mailboxes in the same Outlook profile.

A mailbox can have multiple e-mail addresses (known as **aliases**) associated with it, and those aliases can be from different domains. So you probably have you@yourfirmname.com but you may also have info@yourfirmname.com. You may also be lucky enough to have you@yourpracticearea.com and you@coollaw-yerdomainame.com. If so, all of those addresses can point at the same Exchange mailbox. Another important concept to under-stand, though, is the idea of the **default address**. In Exchange, that's the address that your mailbox will send *from* by default. In most cases, that will be you@yourfirmname.com. Sending from the other addresses also is possible...but it takes a surprising bit of advanced setup to make it happen.

Figure 4.1 illustrates multiple e-mail addresses feeding into the same mailbox. I used the double-arrow to highlight the default address in this example.

Figure 4.1   The Mailbox Is the Center of It All

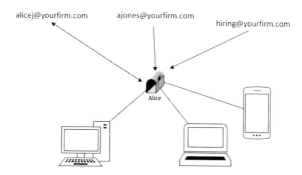

I also used Figure 4.1 to show that multiple kinds of client devices—desktop computers, laptops, tablets, and smartphones—can all connect to a mailbox and send *and* receive information through it. Which brings us to....

Clients

In Exchange nomenclature a client is a piece of software that accesses an Exchange mailbox, and the variety of these clients is actually pretty wide.

Outlook

The best-known of the Exchange clients is Microsoft Outlook, which we discussed in Chapter 3. Outlook has grown up with Exchange and has always been Microsoft's premier Exchange client. To connect to Exchange, Outlook uses advanced protocols that ensure fast and seamless connectivity for synchronizing not only e-mail, but also calendar, contacts, and tasks as well. There are Outlook clients for both Windows and Mac. It's important to note that you'll need at least Outlook 2007 to use it with Office 365 Exchange.

I have a client who was running Office 2003 on some of its computers and didn't want to spend the money to upgrade them when moving to Office 365 Exchange Only. The client's solution was for the users of those computers to access their mailboxes via Outlook Web Access instead. It wasn't perfect, but it was an acceptable workaround.

Setting up Outlook to connect to an Office 365 Exchange mailbox is simple, though, it depends a bit upon the circumstances you're setting it up in. Let's take a look at the three most common scenarios:

BRAND NEW OUTLOOK

This is a new machine, or you've just never used Outlook on this machine before. This is the simplest scenario for setting up Outlook because when you start Outlook for the first time, it will ask if you want to add an e-mail account to it. Click **Yes** and Outlook will ask for your e-mail address and password. Give it that information, and Outlook will use your e-mail address to look for what's called an **Autodiscover record** for your domain. (We'll talk more about Autodiscover records in Chapter 7.) The Autodiscover record points Outlook at the server that contains your configuration information. Using that information, Outlook automatically will set up the Exchange service to connect to Office 365, set up the local copy of the mailbox, and start to download any mail, calendar, contacts, or task items that are already in your Exchange mailbox.

EXISTING OUTLOOK WITH A NEW PROFILE

If you've been using Outlook, but want to make a clean switch to Office 365, the most reliable solution is to create a new Outlook profile containing only the Office 365 mailbox. The exact steps vary slightly depending on the version of Windows you're using, but essentially with Outlook closed go to **Control Panel** in Windows and find the **Mail** applet.

Start the mail applet and click **Show Profiles** as you see in Figure 4.2. Then click the **Add** button, and you'll be prompted to create a new profile. From here, you can use essentially the same steps as for a brand new Outlook installation. Enter how you'd like your name to appear in the name field. Give it your e-mail address and password (twice), and Windows will seek out the Autodiscover record we talked about above, find your configuration information, and set up the profile for you.

Tip: If you don't see the mail applet listed right away, click in the **search box** at the top right corner and type mail. Windows will quickly find the applet for you.

Figure 4.2   Creating a New Profile

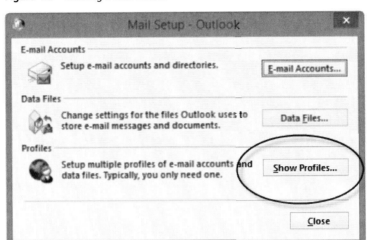

The last step you need to take has to do with how Outlook starts. In Figure 4.3, you see the **Always use this profile option**. You have two choices here:

1. **Always Use: Office 365.** Set that field to the new Office 365 profile that you just created, and Outlook will just start with Office 365 every time.

2. **Prompt for Profile.**
   Each time you start Outlook, it will ask which profile you want to use during that session. This is handy if you think you'll be switching back and forth from another e-mail system and Office 365 fairly often.

Figure 4.3   Choose Which Profile Outlook Uses

EXISTING OUTLOOK WITH THE EXISTING PROFILE

If you've been using Outlook and simply want to add Office 365 to your existing Outlook profile, this is the option for you. Most often we see this choice when the attorney has a personal Gmail or other account and wants to add Outlook to that profile. The downside of this type of setup has two parts: 1) if the existing profile has problems (which it may or may not), the problems may continue when you add Office 365; 2) having multiple e-mail accounts in the same profile can be a slight performance drag. However, you can't beat the convenience if you have multiple accounts you need to stay on top of.

To add Office 365 to an existing Outlook profile, just go to **File** and click **Add Account** at the top left of the Info pane (see Figure 4.4).

Figure 4.4   Adding a New Account to an Outlook Profile

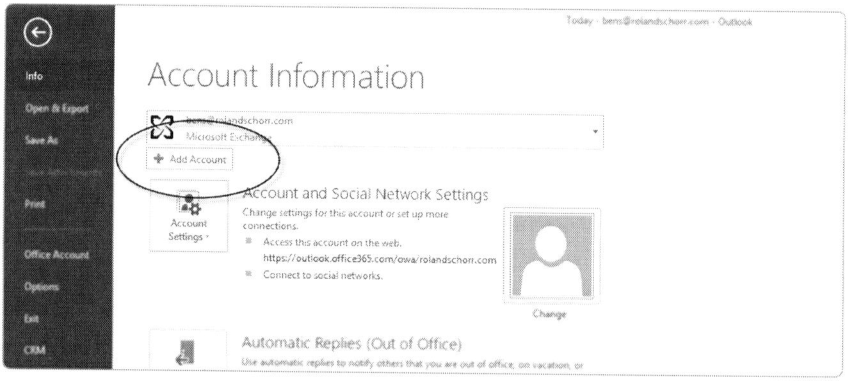

Give the wizard your name as you want it to appear, e-mail address, and Office 365 password, and it should automatically connect and set up your mailbox for you. When you return to Outlook, you should see your Office 365 mailbox listed on the navigation pane along with your previously configured e-mail accounts.

Windows Phone

Naturally one of the best mobile clients for Office 365 Exchange is the Windows Phone—currently on version 8.1. Setting up the Windows Phone for Office 365 is pretty easy; simply go to your apps list, find and start **Office** (which is a built-in app on Windows Phone 8), and click **Office 365 > Setup** on the **Places** screen. Click **Add an Account** and choose **Outlook**. Enter your Office 365 username (e-mail address) and your Office 365 password, and the device should take care of the rest by itself.

You'll probably want to check the box marked **Keep me signed in** by the way. Otherwise, your device will frequently ask you to log back into Office 365.

Android and iOS

Android smartphones and tablets, iPhones, and iPads all have native applications that have been written to use Exchange ActiveSync to connect to an Exchange mailbox.

Setting up a modern Android or iOS device couldn't be much easier. On the Android devices simply go to **Settings > Accounts and sync > Add Account > Email**. When prompted, enter your e-mail address and your Office 365 password. When prompted for the type of account, choose **Microsoft Exchange ActiveSync** (Note: Some devices might just say **Exchange** or **Corporate**). Most Android devices will use the Autodiscover record we talked about earlier to get all of the settings they need, and they'll configure the account for you.

On the next screen (see Figure 4.5), the Android will allow you to select which folders you want synced and whether you want to be notified when new mail arrives. If you don't want something to sync (like Calendar or Contacts), you can uncheck those settings here.

Figure 4.5   Android Account Options

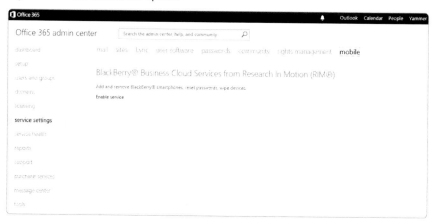

If you have an older Android device, it's possible that it will ask you for your domain and your server name. You should be able to leave domain blank, but for server you'll want to enter **m.out-look.com**. If at any point in this process the device asks for your username, remember that your Office 365 username is always your full e-mail address, e.g., you@yourfirmname.com.

Setting up the iPhone is essentially the same process. Go to **Settings > Mail, Contacts, Calendars**, and add an account. On the iPhone it will usually be called **Microsoft Exchange** or **Corporate**. Enter your e-mail address (username) and Office 365 password (you can leave Domain blank), and the iPhone should find and create your account for you.

If you have an older iPhone it might ask for your server name—give it **m.outlook.com**.

Note that when you set up one of these devices, you may see on the device screen a page that advises that setting up this e-mail grants Microsoft Exchange the ability to control many of the security settings on your device. This is a warning about Exchange's mobile device management capabilities, which we'll talk more about in Chapter 7. Once a device is connected to your Office 365 Exchange server, you do have the ability, from the Office 365 portal, to remotely wipe the device, to require encryption, and to require a password be set on the device.

BlackBerry

If yours is one of the shrinking number of firms that still have BlackBerry devices, then you'll be pleased to know that you can access Exchange server from a Blackberry.

The newest BlackBerry devices use Exchange ActiveSync, just like the Android and iOS devices do, in order to access the mailboxes. Older Blackberry devices may still need to connect to a **BlackBerry Enterprise Server** to connect to Exchange. In that event, it's somewhat more complicated to set up and maintain but it can be done. Before you commit to it, you might want to consider if it would be easier and cheaper to encourage those users to upgrade to newer BlackBerry devices or to another kind of smartphone.

To enable older BlackBerry devices, log into your Office 365 portal at http://portal.office365.com and click **Service Settings** on the left (See Figure 4.6). On the tabs across the top, click **Mobile** and you should see **BlackBerry Business Cloud Services from Research In Motion (RIM)**. Click **Enable Service**, review the Terms and Conditions, and click through the wizard to get to the **RIM Tenant Provisioning** portal. There you can create users and policies, reset passwords, and remotely wipe devices if necessary.

As older BlackBerry devices get retired and go out of service, this tool becomes less and less necessary. At the moment, I have only one client left who still needs to use it, and the

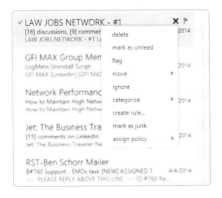

Figure 4.6 Adding an Account to an Older BlackBerry

client is down to only two users who are still carrying the old BlackBerry devices. Maybe by the time this book goes to print, we'll have convinced those users to upgrade.

Outlook Web Access

If you want to access your Exchange mailbox from a computer, but you don't have Outlook installed on that machine—or perhaps it's not your machine, so you don't have an Outlook profile created for you on it—you can use Outlook Web Access to get to the mailbox from any web browser.

To access OWA, just open any web browser and go to http://mail.office365.com. Log in with your e-mail address and Office 365 password, and you'll get a screen that, as of this writing, looks something like Figure 4.7.

Figure 4.7　Outlook Web Access

You'll notice that it looks a bit like Microsoft Outlook, the desktop application we talked about in Chapter 3. Indeed it does. You can see all of your folders on the navigation pane at the left; you can read and reply to your messages and compose new messages. The **Reply**, **Reply All**, and **Forward** buttons are at the top right, and the **New Mail** button to create a new message is at the top left.

As you select each message on the message list, you'll notice that the message appears in the reading pane at the right. To delete a message, click the red **X** that appears to the right of the message on the message list, or just press the **Delete** key on your keyboard when that item is selected.

One interesting user interface feature of modern Outlook Web Access is that you can actually right-click on items in your browser and get an Outlook context menu (see Figure 4.8). That lets you quickly take actions with those items.

The rest of the interface of OWA is a little disjointed. To get to your **Calendar** or **Contacts** (which OWA, like Outlook, now refers to as **People**), you click the links on the navigation bar across the top of the window. To get to your **Tasks**, however, you click Tasks at the bottom left corner of the window.

Figure 4.8 The Outlook Web Access Context Menu

To return to e-mail from any of those screens you click **Outlook** on the navigation bar at the top.

You can do a fair bit of configuration to the way OWA works and looks. To access these options, click on the **Settings** icon (it looks like a gear; see Figure 4.9) at the top right corner of the screen.

To be honest, some of the options on this menu aren't really that useful. The very first item listed is **Refresh**, which is only slightly better than pressing **F5** on your keyboard or clicking the refresh button on your browser. It's slightly better in that it only refreshes the mailbox and not the entire browser window.

The second and fourth items on the list (**Set automatic replies** and **Manage apps**) are just shortcuts to things you'll find under the seventh thing on the list (**Options**).

Display Settings (see Figure 4.9) opens a spacious window that gives you some limited control over how OWA looks. If you have an older web browser or perhaps a very slow Internet connection, you might select the last tab on the list, **Outlook Web App version**, and switch **OWA** into **OWA Light**, which is a simplified version of the site. Other items in this dialog box let you control where (and if) the Reading Pane appears and whether you want the newest messages to appear at the top of the list or at the bottom of the list.

Figure 4.9   The Settings Menu

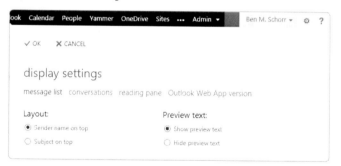

Offline Settings (see Figure 4.10) opens an even more sparsely populated window that lets you turn on (or off) offline access with OWA. Offline access is a new feature with Exchange 2013, and it lets you do most of the things you do when OWA is online, but it lets you do them even when you don't have an Internet connection. Granted there aren't too many times these days when we don't have an Internet connection available, but for those who do run across that issue and rely upon OWA to access their Exchange mailbox, offline access may just be the ticket.

Figure 4.10   OWA Offline Settings

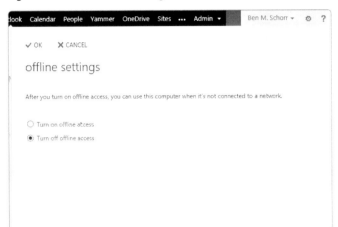

Two caveats to offline OWA mode however:

- In offline mode you can't, as should be obvious, actually send any of those replies or new e-mails you compose. That requires an Internet connection, so the messages you prepare will sit in the OWA outbox waiting to go until you reconnect to the Internet.

- Less obvious: you can't search or sort e-mails while you're in offline mode.

The **Change Theme** option doesn't do quite as much as you might help. Mostly it changes how the very top of the window appears by letting you apply a strip of colored "wallpaper" across it. Adds a little variety, but doesn't do much to change the overall look of the site.

The **Options** dialog is where all the action is for configuring OWA. Figure 4.11 shows you the default page of the Options screen.

Figure 4.11   OWA Options

The first page, **Account**, mostly gives you some basic information about the account you're looking at: display name, e-mail
address, mailbox usage, that sort of thing. On the right side of the
screen are some useful shortcut links to things like **Change your
password** or **Set up an automatic reply message** for times you
want people to get an automatic response when they e-mail you.

Almost unnoticed at the top of that window you can switch
from **my account** to **connected accounts**. Choosing connected
accounts lets you pull your e-mail from other accounts (like
Gmail) into your Outlook Web Access mailbox where you can deal
with it all in one place. The other useful option on the connected
accounts tab is the ability to set up forwarding so you can have all
of the mail you receive on this Exchange mailbox automatically
forwarded somewhere else…such as your Gmail account if that's
what you want.

> **Caution:** If you set up forwarding in this way, it means
> every message sent to your Exchange mailbox will be for-
> warded to the address you specify. If you receive any sensitive
> messages in this mailbox, you can imagine the potential for
> calamity if you forward that mail, intentionally or acciden-
> tally, to a mailbox that somebody other than you has access
> to. Don't forward casually.

External Contacts

Perhaps you want some people to be in your firm's global address list even though they don't have mailboxes in your organization. There are a couple of reasons why you might want to do this, and we'll look at perhaps the most common reason in just a moment. Fortunately, it's easy to add external contacts to your Office 365 account. Since external contacts do not have mailboxes in your organization you might suspect that it doesn't cost you any extra to have them...and you'd be right.

An external contact exists in your global address list, making it easy for your users to send the contact even though he or she doesn't have an @yourfirmname.com e-mail address (though there is a trick to getting an external contact such an e-mail address, and we'll cover it in a minute).

To create an external contact, log into your Office 365 portal click **users and groups**, and above the list of users, you'll see a somewhat jumbled block of commands among which you'll find **Manage email contacts**. (See Figure 4.12.)

Figure 4.12 Users and Groups

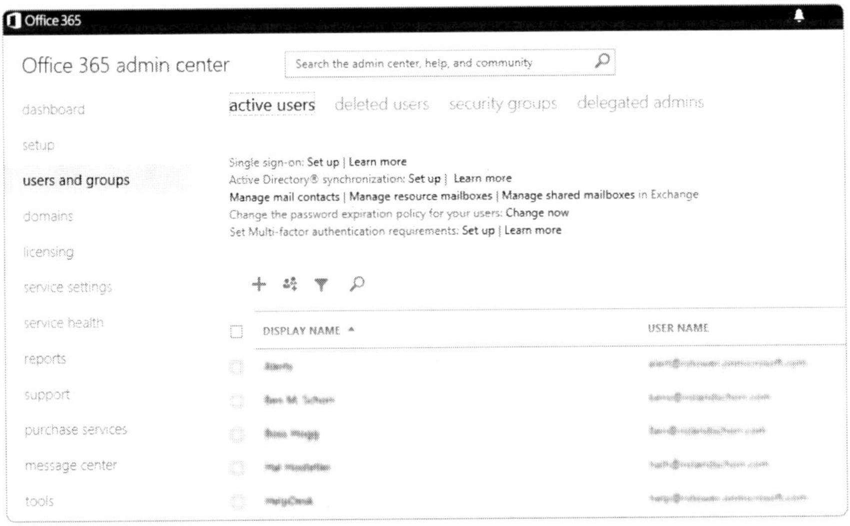

You'll get the Manage Contacts screen you see in Figure 4.13.

Figure 4.13   Manage Contacts

To add a new contact, click the **+ sign** and choose **Mail Contact**. You'll get the Mail Contact form you see in Figure 4.14.

Enter the contact's name in the appropriate fields, give it a display name (or accept the default), and assign an alias to the contact. The alias is what the mail contact can be referred to in your system. So, for example, if you have an outside bookkeeper, you could add him or her as an external contact. Perhaps the outside bookkeeper is "dana@fictionalbookkeeper.co". You could give the bookkeeper the alias of **Bookkeeper**.

Finally, enter the bookkeeper or other contact's external e-mail address (i.e., dana@fictionalbookkeeper.co) and click **Save**.

Now if anybody in your firm wants to send an e-mail to Dana the fictional bookkeeper, they need only type **bookkeeper** in the **TO** field, and the message will go to her at her regular e-mail address.

Groups

Another important feature of Exchange is the ability to create Groups (aka **Distribution Lists**). A group is a collection of mailboxes (and, potentially, external contacts) that has an e-mail alias in your system. Any message sent to that alias will go to everybody in the group.

Figure 4.14   Creating a New Mail Contact

Figure 4.15   Create a New Distribution Group

There are two kinds of distribution groups for you to choose from. The **standard distribution group** has a static list of members, which you can manually add to (or remove from) as users come and go. The **dynamic distribution group** is created "on the fly" based on characteristics in the user accounts.

To create a group, go to **users and groups**, click **security groups** from the navigation list near the top of the window, and select **Manage distribution groups** on the window that appears. Let's take a look at how to create a standard distribution group first, since this is the type of group that most firms actually use. Click the **+ sign** and select **distribution group** to get the new distribution group window (see Figure 4.15).

Give your group a display name and an alias that internal users can use to refer to the group. Perhaps you're creating a distribution group for your Workman's Comp practice area. You might give it the display name of **Workman's Comp Group** and an alias of **WorkComp**. Under e-mail address, you want to give it a unique address in your domain, perhaps **workcomp@yourfirm-name.com**. Description is optional.

In the owners section, click the **+ sign** and select any users in your firm who should be authorized to administer this group—adding and removing members, primarily. Your own name should appear by default.

The next section is the meat of it—the members. Click the **+ sign** to add members as you see in Figure 4.16. Note that you can add both mailboxes in your organization *and* external contacts. That means if you have an of-counsel who does a lot of work comp work with you and you want them to also receive mail addressed to the group, you can add them—assuming you've created an external contact for them, as we discussed in the previous section.

When you've finished adding members, click **Save**. You can always come back in and edit the list of members later, and for a long-standing group you undoubtedly will eventually.

To create a dynamic distribution group, you start the same way as a standard group but instead of selecting Distribution Group to add, select **Dynamic Distribution Group**. In the Dynamic Distribution Group dialog box you see in Figure 4.17, give the group a display name and alias. Remember the alias is the e-mail address

Tricks of the Pros

Want to have an internal address (@yourfirmname.com) map (connect) to an outside address—such as for an of counsel? Create an external contact for that external address. Then create a distribution group with that internal address and make the external contact the only member of that group.

this group is going to receive mail on. You can enter an optional description (I encourage it) and then specify the owner of the group.

The next section is where you control who will be a member of this group. Generally speaking, I leave **All recipient types** selected: less room for error if you do that. Selecting specific recipient types is handy if you feel you need to exclude certain kinds of recipients (like external contacts) but most of the time that's not necessary.

Finally, click **add a rule** to specify the rules that will determine who will be in this group. You can select from a dozen or so different user fields (including a collection of fields that you can set to be anything you want) and specify the text that will have to match in order for the user to be considered part of this group. When you're done setting those rules up, click **Save**.

There is a way to bulk-create distribution groups, just like bulk-creating users,

Figure 4.16 Add Members to the Group

Figure 4.17 Creating a Dynamic Distribution Group

from a **.CSV** (Comma Separated Value) file, but unfortunately, it requires using **PowerShell**—which is a command-line interface that end users don't usually want to get involved with. Your Microsoft Partner or perhaps your IT support folks should be able to help you with that if you have a lot of distribution groups that need to be created at once.

If you want this distribution group to accept e-mail from outside senders, there is one more thing you're going to have to do. After you've saved the distribution group, select it, and click the pencil above the list; that's the **edit** button. You'll get a Distribution Group dialog that looks different from the one you used to create the distribution group to begin with (see Figure 4.18). Click **delivery management** on the left side navigation pane, and you'll get the option to control who this group will accept messages from. By default, the group will only accept messages from senders inside your organization. Click the radio button for **Senders inside and outside of my organization** to enable the group to receive mail from outside.

Figure 4.18   Control Who Can Send to Your Distribution Group

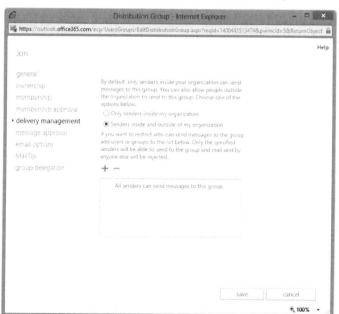

Encrypting E-mail

All of your Exchange data is encrypted between your client (Outlook or mobile) and the Office 365 Exchange server. It's also encrypted while it's sitting on the Exchange server. By extension, any mail you send people in your firm—since it's always on that Exchange server or transiting to or from Outlook—is encrypted. However, you may want to send an encrypted e-mail to an outside party as well. There are several ways to do it, but I'm going to briefly mention two options here.

Exchange Hosted Encryption (Soon to Be Office 365 Message Encryption)

Microsoft offers a server-side, policy-based encryption solution that lets you encrypt any message sent to any party. You create transport rules on the server side that automatically encrypt messages if they meet certain criteria (such as being sent to or from particular people or containing certain key words in the subject line). The person on the other end receives a regular e-mail message indicating that you've sent them an encrypted message. The e-mail has an attachment to click so the recipient can read that message. After clicking the attachment, the browser opens, and the recipient is asked to log in with a free Microsoft account. If the recipient doesn't have one, he or she will be prompted to create one the first time—after that it should be automatic.

Once the recipient successfully authenticates, he or she will be able to read the encrypted message. If the recipient replies to the message, the reply is also encrypted.

Since Exchange Hosted Encryption is server-based, it works regardless of what client you send the e-mail message from. You can send from Outlook, OWA, iPad, Android phone…it doesn't matter. As long as the message meets the policy criteria you specified in the transport rule, the message will be encrypted. It also means that as long as your message meets the rule, the encryption is automatic—you can't forget to click the **Encrypt** button.

If you have an E-3 or E-4 plan, you get this encryption service for free. With the other Enterprise plans, including Exchange-only and Kiosk plans, you'll need to buy the Azure Rights Management service for $2/mailbox/month.

S/MIME

S/MIME (Secure/Multipurpose Internet Mail Extensions) is a method to send secure e-mail messages. It has been around since 1995 and made its Outlook debut in Outlook 97. It's still available, in its updated version, in Outlook 2013. S/MIME uses public-key encryption to securely sign and encrypt your e-mail messages.

Once you have a certificate, you go to (in Outlook) **File > Options > Trust Center > Trust Center Settings > E-mail Security** to get the dialog box you see in Figure 4.19.

Figure 4.19   Trust Center

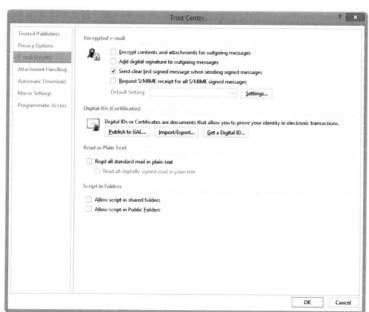

Click **Import/Export** to import your digital certificate. Once you've completed that process, you can encrypt an e-mail message by starting an e-mail to somebody, then clicking **File** > **Properties** in that e-mail message to get to the Properties dialog box you see in Figure 4.20.

Figure 4.20   E-mail Properties

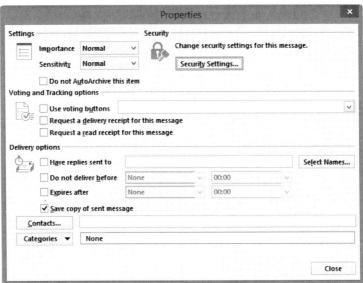

Caution: Geek Content Ahead!

Public-key encryption uses a combination of two separate keys to encrypt the message. You have a **public key**, which you can publish freely, and a **private key**, which you keep very secret. When you want to send an encrypted e-mail to somebody you encrypt it using a combination of your private key and the other person's public key. When they receive the message, they decrypt it using a combination of their private key and your public key. Only the right pair of keys will decrypt the message.

There are tools that will let you generate your own key pairs or, for added security, you can obtain a key pair from one of the well-established Certificate Authorities like **Verisign** or **Thawte**.

Click the **Security Settings** button to get the **Security Proper-ties** dialog box and check the box for **Encrypt message contents and attachments.** Then **OK/Close** your way back out, and your message should be set for encryption.

One catch...you have to already have the other person's public key attached to their contract record in your Contacts. Once you've got that person's public key—either as an attachment or a download, typically, go to his or her contact record in Outlook's people record, and click **Certificates** on the **Ribbon.** Click the **Import** button on the right and import their public key file to their contact record.

Now you're ready to send them S/MIME encrypted e-mail.

What You Need to Know

An Exchange Server hosts mailboxes that contain e-mail, calen-dar, contacts, tasks, and more. It's an enterprise-grade system that now, thanks to Office 365, is available to small and solo firms at a reasonable price. You can use your own domain names with Exchange server and have anywhere from one to thousands of mailboxes on the system. You can access your Exchange data from Microsoft Outlook on the PC or Mac or from virtually any kind of modern mobile device: smartphones or tablets predominantly. Outlook Web Access is the web-based client that Exchange server offers so that you can access your data from any device that has a web browser and an Internet connection.

You can have multiple e-mail addresses and multiple domain names on the same Exchange mailbox and you easily can share your Exchange data, such as your Inbox or your Calendar, with anybody else in your organization.

There are several ways to encrypt e-mail: either with a server-based/policy-based solution that works from any client, or from a more client-centric public key encryption system such as S/MIME.

Finally, you can create external users to send e-mail to and distribution groups that let multiple people inside and outside your firm receive mail sent to the same address.

Chapter 5

SharePoint

Out of all of the Office 365 calls I get perhaps no product generates more questions than SharePoint. Firms are intrigued by its powerful document management and extranet capabilities but aren't quite sure if they'll be able to make use of it. Even colleagues of mine at Microsoft find the question "What is SharePoint?" a difficult one to answer succinctly. So you can imagine my trepidation at trying to answer that question adequately in just fifteen pages or so.

SharePoint is Microsoft's document management, collaboration, and workflow platform. You use it to build Intranet, Extranet, and web portals. It's basically a website to let firms share documents, information, schedules, tasks, and more. Typically accessed through a web browser, it allows you to create and manage document libraries, lists, and sites that you can share internally with your entire firm, with selected practice areas, or even externally with clients or colleagues. The vast majority of SharePoint use is internal—most of my clients who are using SharePoint have never shared any SharePoint content outside of their own firms.

SharePoint online can be especially powerful for firms with multiple locations or lots of mobile users as a capable, Cloud-based platform that can be accessed anyplace with Internet access.

Entire books, far thicker than this one, have been written about SharePoint, so in this chapter, I'll touch on the highlights and try to answer the questions about it I get most often from law firms.

Sites

The centerpiece of SharePoint is the **site collection**. A site collection consists of a top-level site and any subsites of that top-level site you might choose to create. You don't have to create subsites, but you can. Sites in Office 365 are often referred to as **Team Sites**. A Team Site is, as the name implies, a site you can create and share with your entire team—including team members who are not in your organization if you like. Your team can use Team Sites to share documents, communicate, and collaborate on a project—and with Office 365, those SharePoint Team Sites are on SharePoint.com, which means they're cloud-hosted and available anywhere you have an Internet connection.

You can create multiple Team Sites in SharePoint. You can have separate sites for each practice area in your firm, for example, or you might even create a separate site for a big case. When you first sign into your Office 365 SharePoint Team Site, it will be clean, out of the box. If you'd like to create a new subsite—for example, maybe you're going to create a special Team Site for a particular practice area in your firm—that's easy to do. Click the **Sites** link on the **Quick Launch** pane at the left, and scroll down the page. You'll see the **new subsite** button (see Figure 5.1) and you can create one or more custom subsites.

Figure 5.1   Creating New Subsites

There are a number of different elements—referred to as **Apps** in SharePoint—that can comprise a SharePoint Team Site, and you can choose which of them you want and how you want them to look. You can even brand them with your firm logo if you like.

Document Libraries

One of the most common kinds of elements that firms include in a Team Site is a document library—a hosted "folder" that contains documents of all types. You can create multiple document libraries, and you can share those document libraries not only with team members within your firm, but also with parties outside your firm.

A document library can be divided into subfolders, and you can share those subfolders with different users. For example, you could have a library called Clients, and you could divide that into subfolders for different matters and share each subfolder only with the paralegal or associates who are working on that particular matter.

To create a new document library, click the **settings button** (looks like a gear) at the top right of the screen and then click **add an app**. On the list of apps that appears (see Figure 5.2), select **Document Library** to create a new library. Give your library a name, and click **Create**—that's all there is to getting a new library started.

Figure 5.2   Adding an App

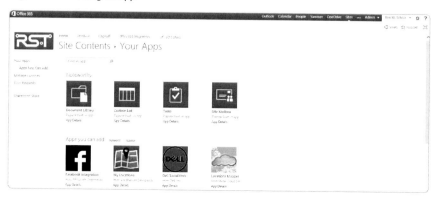

VERSIONING

One of the more useful features of SharePoint document libraries isn't even enabled by default, and that's the ability to keep track of multiple versions of a document. I strongly encourage firms to enable this feature. I can't tell you how many times I've gotten panicked calls from a firm because one of their users overwrote an important document with a flawed version, and they wanted me to help them restore the old version. If you don't have versioning enabled, that can mean hoping that you have a backup or another copy of the older version somewhere.

To enable versioning, go into the document library and click the **Library** tab at the top of the **Ribbon**. On that tab—which you can see in Figure 5.3—click the **Library Settings** button, which is toward the right end of the ribbon.

Figure 5.3   The Library Tab of the Ribbon

On the **Settings** screen (see Figure 5.4), you'll see Versioning Settings. Click that to get the **Versioning Settings** screen you see in Figure 5.5.

Figure 5.4   The Settings Screen

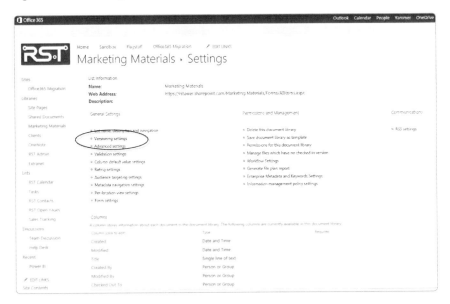

Figure 5.5   Versioning Settings

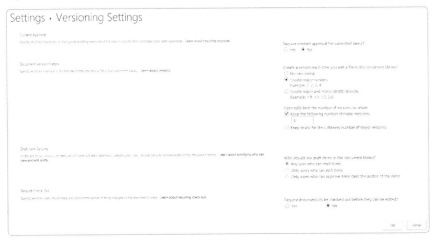

SharePoint has the ability not only to keep multiple versions of a document but also to distinguish between a document that is in draft state, version approved, or final state. Some firms use that if paralegals or associates are drafting initial versions of documents that have to be subsequently approved by more senior attorneys in the firm.

On the Versioning Settings page you can enable **Require content approval for submitted items** as a key step toward creating a workflow that would place any submitted documents in that library in draft stage until approved by an authorized person.

Workflow and approval is a somewhat more advanced topic than we have the space to dig into here, however. For our purposes, the settings on this page that are interesting are the **Create a version...** settings. By default, it's set to **No versioning** but you can change that to have SharePoint create major and/or minor versions of your documents when you make changes.

In SharePoint terms a **workflow** is the automated movement of documents or items through a sequence of actions or tasks as part of a business process. For example: the drafting of a standardized document might start with a paralegal, then go to an associate for more detailed work, and finally go to a reviewing partner for final approval. SharePoint workflows can help move the document through the process with notifications to the required participants and updated status on the document as it happens.

SharePoint workflows can be heavily customized, and they can be powerful tools for larger firms with a lot of fairly standardized collaboration tasks.

Typically, I'll enable major versions, and then on the next part I'll tell SharePoint to keep three major versions. You can season those settings to taste, of course.

If you have both major and minor versions enabled, keep in mind that SharePoint will, by default, save new versions as minor versions unless you manually designate a particular version as a major version. For most firms, a major version is a version that is ready to be reviewed by a large group, while a minor version is likely a draft that somebody is working on. For example, if you go through three revisions of a document before you're ready to submit it to the client for review, we might say that your first two revisions are versions 1.1 and 1.2 and the third version—the one you're going to send along—is version 2.0. If the client returns the document with comments, you might check their version in as 2.1, and then continue from there.

FORCING FIELDS

One of the features common to document management systems is the ability to designate certain profile information as mandatory. You can do that in SharePoint as well. You can go to the **document library** and click the **Library** tab on the **Ribbon** then click **Library Settings**, and you'll see the list of columns part way down the page. You can click on the title of any column to edit it and you can set that column as **required**—i.e., it can't be blank.

Some firms will choose to add Client # and Matter # columns to the library and set them as required. Anybody saving a document to that document library will be required to provide client and matter numbers to identify the document.

Calendars

Another very common request firms have is creating a centralized firm calendar the entire firm can share and that is separate from anyone's personal calendars. SharePoint gives you the ability to do that quite easily. When I tell firms that, the next thing I hear, usually, is "We don't want to have to log into a website to see our firm calendar." Good news—you don't have to. In fact, you can easily integrate your SharePoint calendar(s) into Outlook.

To add a calendar to your SharePoint team site, click the **settings button** at the top right corner, and select **Add an app**. Find the Calendar app, give it a name, and add it. When the calendar appears in your Team Site you can add items to it and interact with it like any other calendar. You can even change the view from Month to Day to Week if you like.

If you want to link that calendar to Outlook, click the **Calendar** tab of the **Ribbon** as you can see in Figure 5.6 (it only appears when the calendar is selected, so make sure you've clicked somewhere in the calendar), and choose **Connect to Outlook**. A short wizard will run confirming that you wish to open the calendar in Outlook, and when it's done, this calendar will be added as an additional calendar.

Figure 5.6   The Calendar Tab of the Ribbon

Anything you add to the calendar in Outlook or in SharePoint will be reflected in the other site as well. This is the system we use at Roland Schorr & Tower for maintaining our firm calendar, and I rarely go into the calendar on our SharePoint site. I use it almost exclusively from Outlook on my desktop or on my laptop.

One of the questions I get a lot is about syncing the SharePoint calendars to mobile devices. The answer to that one is...there isn't an easy way to do it. Some platforms have third-party tools that claim to integrate with SharePoint. The ones I've seen so far don't seem very reliable. Naturally you can open your SharePoint site (and its calendar[s]) in the browser on your phone, but that's probably not what you're hoping for. For the moment, we just have to accept that there are workarounds for doing it, but no great solutions yet. We can hope that Microsoft will release an official SharePoint app for the mobile platforms that accesses the calendars more seamlessly.

Contacts

Many of our clients use Contacts as a firm-wide, shared contacts list. You can put in judges, experts, vendors, even clients if you want to. Like the Calendar, it is similarly integrated with Outlook, so you can readily access this information without signing into the Team Site directly.

To create a contacts list, click the **settings button** at the top right, choose **Add an App**, and select the **Contacts app**. Give it a name and create it. The list that SharePoint creates for you is fairly rudimentary and not that pleasant to work with. That said, to connect it to Outlook so you can work with it in Outlook instead, click the **List** tab of the **Ribbon** (see Figure 5.7) and click the "Connect to Outlook" button. Outlook will open that Contacts folder and it will appear just as any other contacts folder in Outlook.

Figure 5.7   The Contacts Tab of the Ribbon

Simple Tasks

You can create a simple task list in SharePoint, indicating the task subject, due date, and even the person who is responsible for it. Some firms will use this feature to create a to-do list of tasks for a matter, including designating the responsible party: on the firm's staff, an outside expert, or even the client.

To add a tasks app to a SharePoint Team Site, click the **settings button** at the top right corner, select **Add an App**, and select the **Tasks app**. Give it a name, and you'll be off and running with your simple tasks list.

Like calendar and contacts, there is a **Sync to Outlook** option on the **List** tab of the **Ribbon** that you can use to sync these tasks with Outlook, where they might be more useful and accessible to you.

One of the rather cool features the simple tasks list has is the **Predecessors** feature. That's where you can specify tasks that need to be completed before a particular task can be completed. To see it, open the task item and click the **Show More** link at the bottom. That's a level of capability that native Outlook tasks don't have (at least not yet).

You can also create custom views of your tasks in SharePoint to mimic the basic functionality of Microsoft Project—with Gantt charts and dependent tasks. Creating a custom view is a bit deep for this book, but I can point you in the right direction. While in the Tasks list, click the **List** tab on the **Ribbon** and then click the **Create View** button. There you have a tremendous number of settings to play with so you can configure your custom view however you like.

Custom Lists

If none of these list types are exactly what you need, you can always create a custom list. Just like any flat file database, you can populate your custom list with any fields that you like.

To create a custom list, click the **settings button** at top right, select **Add an App** and choose **Custom List**. Give your custom list a name, and then you're ready to start creating fields. As with all good database design, it's a good idea to stop and figure out what the list will be used for, what fields you'll need, and how you'll use them before you start creating the list.

I always recommend to clients who are going to play around with SharePoint's settings that they create a subsite called Sandbox where they can safely play while they're learning. Playing with the settings in your production Share-Point site can be a good way to confuse your users and even put your data at risk. Creating a separate subsite that you can play around in is safe because no production data is there and if things go really really badly you can just delete that Sandbox subsite and create a fresh new one.

Quick Launch

The navigation pane at the left side of the screen is called the **Quick Launch bar**, and it is configurable. To add or remove an item, click the **settings button** at the top right of the screen and select **Site Settings**. On the Site Settings page that appears (see Figure 5.8), you'll find **Quick Launch** under the **Look and Feel** section in the right-hand column.

Figure 5.8 Site Settings

Not only can you edit or rename any of the links that are there, but you can add others. For example: you could choose to add links to your firm's public website or to LexisNexis or to the local court websites or…

You can even choose to turn the Quick Launch bar off entirely if you just really don't want to see it.

Search

One of the strengths of SharePoint is its capability to search. You can search for content—documents, workbooks, or more. You can also search for keywords in online discussions or e-mails. Perhaps you have an image library where the images have been tagged with particular keywords to help you find them.

SharePoint offers you a search field right at the top right corner of the screen. Type any word or phrase, and SharePoint can search across your entire Team Site for documents, images, notes, slide decks, and other materials that match. One of Share-Point's really powerful features is that it will even search *within* certain kinds of documents. If you have a Word document, for example, and the terms you're searching for appear within the Word document, SharePoint search will surface that document and even show you the context in which that term appears (see Figure 5.9).

On the left side of the results is a refinement panel that lets you narrow down your search results to a particular document type or perhaps a particular author.

Figure 5.9   Finding Terms Inside Documents

Discussions

One web part that can be very powerful in a team site is the **Discussions** app. Add it by clicking the **settings button** at the top right corner, select **Add an App** and find **Discussions**. Once you've added that to your site's page, you can start and carry on threaded discussions with all of the other people who access that Team Site. This can be a great way to have a collaborative "group chat" about the project or team. Figure 5.10 shows you a sample discussion.

Figure 5.10   Group Discussions

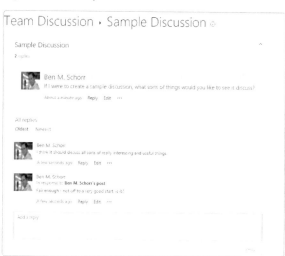

The content of those discussions will even be indexed and featured in search results if appropriate.

Extranets

One of the questions we often get about SharePoint is whether or not you can use SharePoint to collaborate with clients, experts, or co-counsel who are outside your firm. Firms primarily want to be able to share documents with external users, but when they start using SharePoint, they recognize the utility of also sharing task lists, calendars, contacts, and more. So, the answer is yes, but first you have to tick a couple of boxes to make external sharing possible.

To share a SharePoint site or site collection with external users, you have to enable external sharing. To do that, you have to go to the **SharePoint Administration Portal** by clicking **Admin > SharePoint** from the navigation bar at the very top. In the site collections page, you'll see a list of your site collections like the one you see in Figure 5.11.

Figure 5.11   Manage Site Collections

Click the checkbox in front of the site collection you want to share externally and click the **Sharing** button on the small **Ribbon**. On the sharing dialog box (see Figure 5.12) you'll be able to enable sharing to external users and/or anonymous guest users.

Once you've done that, you can share an individual file, a folder, or just about any element in a SharePoint site (including the site itself) with outside users.

To share the site, click the **Share** button near the top right corner and type the e-mail address(es) of the people you wish to invite to share the site.

Figure 5.12   Enable Sharing to External Users

To share an individual document, library, or app, click the **Library** or **List** tab on the **Ribbon** and choose **Shared With** from the Ribbon. Type the e-mail addresses of the people you wish to invite to share that library or app.

To share an individual file in a document library, select the file and click the **"3 dots"** button to the right of the file name and select **Shared With**. As with the first two, type the e-mail address(es) of the people you wish to share that file with.

In all of those cases, an e-mail message will be sent to the users whose e-mail addresss you typed inviting them to open whatever it is you're sharing.

OneDrive for Business

If you just want to store a big group of files and don't need all of the fancy functionality of a full-blown SharePoint Team Site, you can use your OneDrive for Business site. Every user gets a OneDrive for Business site, and Microsoft has recently announced that it was bumping up the size of those sites to 1TB (yes, 1 terabyte) of space per user.

To use your OneDrive for Business, just click the **OneDrive** link on the navigation bar at the top. It will look suspiciously like a SharePoint document library, but that's because it basically is. You can store any files you like here, and each file is private by default.

Sharing

If you want to share a file with somebody, just click the **"3 dots"** button after the filename, and choose **Share**. When the share window appears, type the e-mail address(es) of the people you want to share the file with and send. They'll get an invitation to access the document via e-mail.

When you initiate the sharing, you can choose between letting the recipient edit or view the file. That's handy if you want somebody to be able to see or refer to a document but not modify it.

Sync

If you want a copy of your OneDrive for Business folder on your local computer—or if you have a folder on your local computer you would like synced to OneDrive for Business—click the **Sync** button at the top right. If you don't already have the OneDrive for Business app installed on you computer, you'll need to install it. Click the **Get the OneDrive for Business App...** link that you see when you click the Sync button (see Figure 5.13), and you'll be able to download and install it for free.

Figure 5.13 OneDrive Offers You the OneDrive for Business App

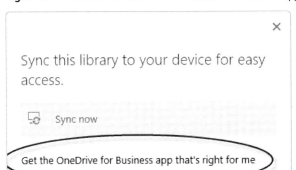

Once that app is installed on your computer, you'll be able to sync any OneDrive for Business folders that you want to your local computer.

Office Web Apps

If you're using a computer that doesn't have Microsoft Office installed, you can still create, view, and edit Microsoft Office documents in SharePoint or OneDrive for Business. Free web apps are available for Word, Excel, PowerPoint, and OneNote. To use them, just click on a document, workbook, slide deck, or notebook in your SharePoint or OneDrive libraries. The document will, by default, open in the web version of the appropriate application.

To create a new document, click the **New Document** button at the top of your file list, and SharePoint will ask you what kind of document to create (Word, Excel, PowerPoint, OneNote). Make your choice, and a new blank document will appear in your browser, ready to edit. (See Figure 5.14.)

Figure 5.14   A New Blank Word Web App Document

The web apps are somewhat more limited than their desktop counterparts, but they're good enough for quick editing or document creation, and they come in very handy if you happen to be at a machine that isn't your own—like one at an airport kiosk or hotel business center—and need to get some quick work done on a file.

Public Sites

One of the other capabilities that SharePoint offers is the ability to create a public website. If you don't already have a website for your firm, or if you're not happy with the site you have, you could create a new public website in SharePoint. A surprising number of public sites including Ferrari, Chili's (the restaurant chain), and Hawaiian Airlines are actually SharePoint sites.

To get started with your public site, click **Sites** on the navigation bar at the top and then select **Public Site**. You'll find a sample site already created and waiting for you to personalize. You can change the look and add content.

Click the **Site** tab of the **Ribbon** to change the logo, title, and other settings of the site.

On each page, click the **Page** tab of the **Ribbon** and choose **Edit** to make changes to that page. When you're happy with the content of the page, click **Save and Publish**.

You can, of course, use your personalized domain (i.e., www.yourfirmname.com) for your public SharePoint website. To do that, just create a CNAME record in your domain's DNS to point to the URL of your public SharePoint site, which is probably something like http://yourfirmname-public.sharepoint.com.

Yammer

In 2012, Microsoft bought enterprise social networking site Yammer (see Figure 5.15). They've since integrated it into their enterprise-level Office 365 SharePoint plans. Yammer lets you create "networks" of people with whom you can have discussions, share files, conduct polls, post events, and so on. Membership in a Yammer "network" is tightly controlled and easily limited to just people in your firm or people you invite.

Figure 5.15 Yammer

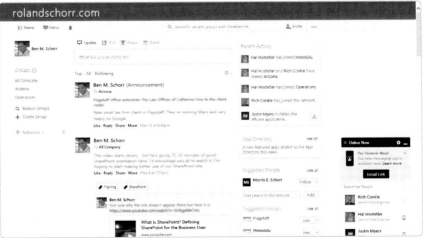

With Yammer, you can create subgroups within your network. Different people in your firm can subscribe to different subgroups, so the discussions are logically separated. You might create separate groups for each practice area, for example.

So far I haven't seen very many firms using Yammer, and I suspect that's because it's (often correctly) viewed as another unnecessary silo for information that firms don't want to have to check and keep up with.

What You Need to Know

SharePoint is Microsoft's document management, collaboration, and workflow platform. It's especially powerful in that it can be heavily customized for project management, client collaboration, and other tasks. You can create calendars, contacts lists, document libraries, and more in the SharePoint site and share them with other users in your firm or even people external to your firm. SharePoint is heavily used by Fortune 500 and AmLaw 100 companies around the world. If you have the time or the money, SharePoint can be customized to do almost anything you want it to do.

OneDrive for Business is the personal file storage tool in SharePoint. Each user gets 1TB of storage space in his or her OneDrive for Business folder and can put almost anything in it. Both OneDrive for Business and SharePoint document libraries can be configured to synchronize to local folders on your computer.

SharePoint Online can also be used to create and publish public websites. Companies like Hawaiian Airlines and the State of Georgia use SharePoint for their public websites.

Yammer is an enterprise-class social networking tool that, by default, is private to your firm. It hasn't really caught on with law firms using Office 365 yet.

Chapter 6

Lync

In recent years, there has been a bit of a push-back on e-mail. Believe it or not, some people feel it's *too* structured and not fast enough. Also, some feel that the temporary nature of an instant messenger (IM) conversation, more akin to a water-cooler chat, is better than cluttering up an inbox with messages that are more informal. As a result, many firms have expanded their use, at least internally, of instant messaging. Also, the popularity of Skype (now owned by Microsoft) has made voice and video calling from the computer a very real choice for many business and home users.

Microsoft's Lync product brings instant messaging and voice and video calling to your business desktop.

When you first set up Lync, only the users in your organization appear in the Lync directory. You can add other contacts, though adding contacts on some other instant messaging systems (like Skype) will require you to enable, for example, Lync to Skype connectivity via something called **Federation**. We'll talk more about that shortly. First, let's take a look at the various ways Lync lets you communicate.

Presence

Lync is a kind of communication known as **synchronous communication**. That means that I reach out to Justin, and he has to respond right then. He responds to me, and I respond to him more or less in real time. Telephone calls are an excellent example of synchronous communication.

Contrast that example to e-mail, a form of **asynchronous communication**. I can send Justin an e-mail message, and he can read it tomorrow morning and reply tomorrow afternoon. I might not see his message for minutes, hours, or days...at which point I can send him a reply. Additionally, e-mail conversations can often span multiple devices. I may send Justin the original e-mail from my desktop, read his reply on my smartphone, and send him a follow-up e-mail the following day from my laptop.

The problem with synchronous communication is that it requires both parties to be available at the same time. Traditionally, you usually had no idea whether the person you were calling was actually available to take your call. Lync (and most

If you happen to send an IM to a user who has wandered away from his or her desk, it will still be waiting when the person returns. You, however, might not be. Thus IM conversations, that are technically synchronous, could become somewhat asynchronous. In my experience, those types of IM chats tend to become pretty frustrating and awkward as each party responds, often hours later. IM is generally used for questions that have a short, quick answer. Most people give up on the IM if they don't get a response fairly promptly.

applications like it) use the concept of "presence" (see Figure 6.1), which means that you tell (directly or indirectly) the application when you're at your desk and available. That information is provided to the people you've accepted as contacts—typically your co-workers.

With the presence information on Lync, you can see if someone is available before you reach out to him or her. In theory that's a great thing—you don't waste time reaching out to somebody who isn't there or who doesn't want to be disturbed. Unfortunately, presence can be surprisingly unreliable. Even though Lync can pull presence information from users' calendars—i.e., automatically flagging them as Busy when they have an appointment scheduled or Away when their calendar shows that or they're out of the office—that information is only as reliable as the users' calendars. Additionally Lync can be configured to show users as Inactive if their computer is idle for some number of minutes, and then show that they are Away after a certain number of additional minutes. In the real world, though, the user might be at his or her desk and even available, though just not actually using the computer for those minutes.

Figure 6.1   Presence Information Helps You to Know Availability

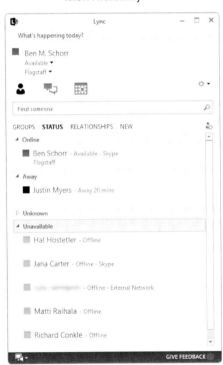

The other problem with presence, and this is not just a Lync problem, is that it's almost entirely at the mercy of the user. It's good that you can set your presence to Do Not Disturb, but the problem is that users frequently set their presence that way and forget they did it—meaning they're on Do Not Disturb for days or even weeks on end. Conversely, in an age when users often don't turn off their computers, the user might be shown as Available when, in fact, he or she is not even at work.

Since presence is well known for being so unreliable, users too often ignore it, negating much of its value. Sending a message to a user who is shown as Away on the off-chance the user is actually available has become commonplace.

To see your current presence status on Lync, just look at the Lync window (see in Figure 6.1). Just below your name, you can see your status. Additionally, to the left of your name, you'll see a small colored box—the color of which indicates your present status (green for available, red for Do Not Disturb, yellow for Away, etc.).

To change your current status, just click the status below your name to expand the status choices as shown in Figure 6.2. Choose the desired status and that's what you've got. Remember though... whatever status you choose is what your status will be until you come back and reset it. If you're particularly mobile, it may become a bit of a chore to stay on top of your actual status.

Another convenient feature of Lync presence information is that it integrates into Outlook. When you get an e-mail from a user who is

Figure 6.2   Choose a Different Status

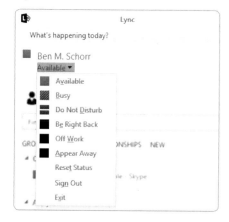

one of your Lync contacts (see Figure 6.3) or you're looking at that user's contact card (see Figure 6.4), the user's current presence status is indicated by the color to the left of their contact picture.

Figure 6.3 Presence Information Integrated into E-mail

Justin is currently shown as Available in Lync. If I click on his contact picture, I can choose to start an instant messenger chat with him, call him using Lync, or start a video call with him. (See Figure 6.5.)

Figure 6.4 Presence Information on the Contact Card

Figure 6.5 Initiating a Lync Call or Instant Messenger Session from Outlook

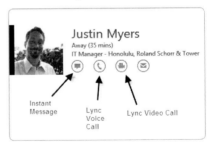

Instant Messaging

Instant messaging is a surprisingly enduring technology. Though it's popularly seen as a tool for teenagers to gossip with each other, it actually dates back to the mid-1960s. At its base, instant messaging is as simple as you can get: two people typing text messages back and forth to each other in a realtime text chat— sort of a computer-based SMS. Over the years, the technology has gotten some enhancement such as nicer fonts and emojis (the little graphical characters such as smiley faces).

As Instant Messaging (IM) systems have gotten more sophisticated, the ability to add multiple parties into the text chat has become common-place. With Lync, you can have up to 250 people in your Lync meeting or chat.

Emoji comes from the Japanese meaning quite literally "picture" *(e)* "chararacter" *(moji)*.

In the office, IM is commonly used in occasions where a quick, informal communication is desired (see Figure 6.6). Frequently, we see firms use IM to have receptionists notify attorneys (and/or their assistants) that a client has arrived for an appointment or to ask a quick question.

Starting an IM chat with a user is a simple matter. Just find the user on your Lync directory and double-click on the person's name. Lync will open an IM chat automatically and you can begin typing. This isn't 1994's instant messenger client though—within Lync's IM chat you can choose to share a whiteboard or show your screen to the other person to collaborate on a document or

Figure 6.6   A Quick Chat on Lync

presentation. You can invite others to the chat or even decide to convert it to a voice or video call. Let's take a quick look at how you do those things.

Whiteboard

Figure 6.7 shows me starting a whiteboard session with Justin, and in Figure 6.8 you can see that whiteboard in action.

Figure 6.7   Starting a Whiteboard Session

Figure 6.8   Using the Whiteboard

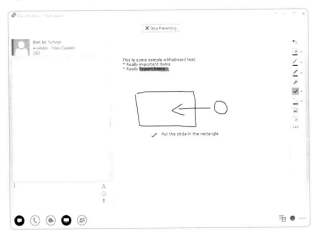

The whiteboard is an electronic version of the board we're all used to seeing in meetings. You can draw on it with electronic ink, insert or paste in images, type text, or take notes that both of you can refer to.

> **Tip:** If you're using your computer for other things during the Lync meeting, you may want to set Lync to be Always on Top so it doesn't accidentally end up in the background during the meeting. To do that, click the **settings button** (looks like a gear, in the top half of the window on the right) highlight **Tools** and then select **Always on Top**.

At any time, you can choose to save the whiteboard as a PNG (image) file, or you can send it to OneNote to make it part of your notes.

Screen Sharing

The same tool that lets you share a whiteboard (see Figure 6.8) also lets you share your screen or even just one program. I have dual monitors on my machine, which is why in my screen shot you can see it offers both Primary Monitor and Secondary Monitor as options. That's handy because it means you can have your notes on one screen, where the other participants don't see them, and whatever you want to share on the other screen.

If you want to keep participants even more focused, you can click **Program** and choose from any of the running programs on your machine. Then the other party will only see what is in that program and not the entire screen—handy if you only have one monitor and want to have your notes on part of the screen while sharing the program on the other.

PowerPoint

If you plan to do a more formal presentation in the meeting and want to show a PowerPoint slide deck, you can choose Power-Point from the sharing options you see in Figure 6.7, and Lync will open a file explorer window so you can locate the slide deck you want to present. Once you open it there, Lync will show the other party the slides as you click through them and present—you don't have to open PowerPoint to make that work.

Transcripts

If you're an Office 365 user, you don't actually have to do anything to save a transcript of your chat. Lync will automatically save it in your Exchange mailbox for you in a folder called Conversation History. There you'll find a full-text, searchable history of all of the instant messenger chats you've had in Lync.

If you want to turn off the transcripts feature, go to Lync and click the **settings button** toward the top right (looks like a gear). Click **Personal** from the navigation pane on the left and uncheck the box for **Save IM conversations in my email Conversation History folder**. You might want to uncheck the **Save call logs...** setting as well, as long as you're here.

Calling

Lync makes it easy to conduct calls with your contacts. Basic voice calls are made in much the same way that you might make a Skype call. You find the person or persons in your directory that you want to call, and double-click their name(s). That will open an IM window but the call button is along the bottom as you can see in Figure 6.9.

Alternatively, you can right-click a name on the directory and select **Call > Lync Call**. Calling via Lync is the same as calling via Skype...and really not much different than calling with a regular phone. It'll ring, if someone is there and wants to answer, you can talk.

Figure 6.9   Making a Voice Call

Lync-to-Lync voice calls have the same sharing capabilities that I described for instant messenger chats: you can share your screen or a whiteboard while you're talking over Lync, too. Just as with an instant messenger session you can add up to 250 people to your Lync call to turn it into a conference call. Be forewarned though, adding that many people consumes additional bandwidth and can quickly turn a productive call into a cacophony.

> If you plan to use Lync for a lot of voice calling, you may want to invest in a good headset. A proper microphone can make an enormous difference in the sound quality, especially if you're in an environment that isn't completely silent.

Calling Regular Phones?

One of the advanced capabilities of Microsoft Lync is the ability to use it as a phone system. Yes, calling and receiving calls from regular telephones, getting voicemail and the whole deal. Lync has the capability of replacing your business **PBX** system. That said, if you want that capability today, you're going to have to subscribe to the E4 plan of Office 365 ($22/mailbox/month currently), and you're going to have to deploy a Lync server on your premises. Lync can serve as a PBX but it does, obviously, require some way to connect to the **PSTN** (Public Switched Telephone Network) in order to send or receive calls from regular telephones.

In 2012, a company called JahJah started offering Lync-to-Phone calling services (for a fee, of course). Unfortunately, the company later announced that it would be shutting down that service as of January 2014. Some people have seen the withdrawal of JahJah from the Lync-to-Phone market as a setback for this functionality, but stay tuned. Microsoft has expressed the goal of significantly enhancing this **Enterprise Voice** capability in Lync later in 2014.

Video Calling

If you find that your calls are enhanced by seeing and being seen by the other person, Lync gives you an easy way to do that. If you double-click the user's name on the directory, then click the movie-camera icon on the bottom row (see Figure 6.10). Lync will initiate a video call with that person.

Figure 6.10   Starting a Video Call

If you want to see how you look before you start the call, just hover over the video call icon and Lync will activate your camera and show you what the other party will see. That's handy if you want to make sure your hair is in place, or that the clutter on your desk is out of camera range or to remind you to get rid of that stack of empty pizza boxes on the credenza behind you.

It should go without saying that you have to have a connected camera in order for video calling to display your image to the other person—and vice versa. Also, the other person will have the option to answer the call without video—meaning that if you catch them in their bathrobe they will see you, but you won't see them. If you initiate a video call and then think better of it, you can always turn off your camera without disconnecting the call. Just click that movie-camera button again, and Lync will let you stop sharing your video.

Doing a video call doesn't require as much bandwidth as most people think it does, but it does require some. Likewise adding screen sharing, whiteboarding, multiple participants... all of that can add to the amount of bandwidth required for the call and may be a drag on call performance. If you find that you're having poor quality audio or video, try simplifying. Often a call that sounds terrible with video enabled sounds much better when the cameras turn off. People always tell me I look better when my camera is turned off, too.

Welcome to the Party—Inviting Others

Whatever kind of connection you're having—IM or voice or video call—you can invite others to join by clicking the **Participants** button on the right end of the bottom row (see Figure 6.11) and then clicking Invite More People. You can select anybody in your Lync directory, or type the address of another Lync user to invite the person to your call or meeting. If you have federa-

Figure 6.11   Inviting Others to the Call

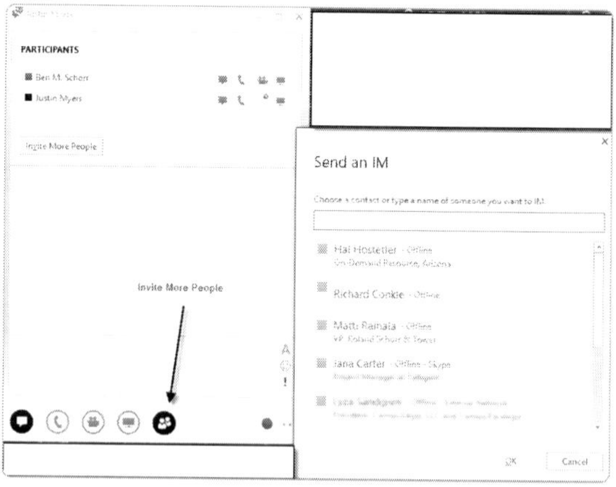

tion turned on to public IM networks like Skype, you can connect to users of those systems as well. "What's federation?" you ask. Glad you asked.

Federation

Federation means associating your system with other systems. With Lync Online in Office 365, you can log into your Office 365 portal at http://portal.office365.com click **Admin** on the top navigation bar and choose **Lync.** On the left side of the screen, select **Organization** and click to the **external communications** tab that you see in Figure 6.12. There you can control whether your Lync users can connect to external networks or not. If you're in a highly regulated industry, or you just want to lock down Lync so that your users can only talk with each other (on Lync at least) during the workday, you may want to block access to other networks. Otherwise, you can enable federation to other networks, including Skype, here.

Figure 6.12   Configuring Federation in Lync

Hosting Meetings and Webinars

Lync is not only powerful for person-to-person communication, you can also host larger meetings and even webinars with it. My firm uses Lync every two weeks for our company-wide meetings.

To invite people to a meeting or a webinar with Lync, the best way is from Outlook. Go to the calendar in Outlook and click **New Lync Meeting** on the **Ribbon** (see Figure 6.13). As with the instant messenger and voice sessions, you're currently limited to 250 attendees in a meeting or webinar.

Figure 6.13 Starting a New Lync Meeting

Fill in the subject of the meeting, specify all of your desired attendees in the TO field, and set the date and time in the appropriate fields. As you can see in Figure 6.14, Outlook already creates a link to the meeting in the notes section of the invite.

Figure 6.14 Creating the Meeting Invite

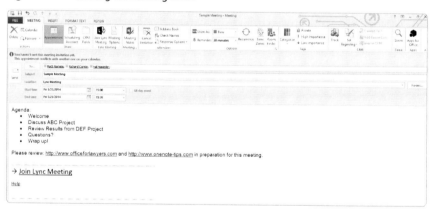

You might choose to add some information to the notes field, such as an agenda for the meeting, additional links or notes the attendees might need, and so on. When you're all set, click **Send**.

When it's meeting time, just click the **Join Lync Meeting** link in the notes field of the appointment, and Lync will automatically connect you to the meeting.

One of the nice things about using Lync for meetings and webinars is that your attendees don't have to be using PCs. In fact, there are Lync clients for Mac, Windows Phone, iPhone, iPad, and Android. You can initiate chats or calls to any or all of those devices.

To take that one step further, your attendees don't even have to be Lync users at all. If you send a meeting or webinar invitation to a person who doesn't have Lync installed or isn't a Lync user, when they click the invite, the person's browser will open and take him or her to a web-based version of Lync! You'll get two-way voice, and they'll be able to see whatever visuals you're sharing with them—whiteboard, screen, PowerPoint slide deck, or something else. Some of my clients use this capability to host webinars for prospective clients on substantive legal topics. The client will prepare a PowerPoint slide deck and invite several dozen prospective clients to "attend."

Saving the Meeting for Later

When you're in the meeting, if you click the **"3 dots"** button at the bottom right corner, the first option that appears is the **Start Recording** option. That lets you record your meeting or webinar, so you can refer to it later or share it with others. Lync will record your meeting in .MP4 format, which plays in most standard video players such as Windows Media Player.

What You Need to Know

Lync is Microsoft's online communication platform. You can use Lync to have secure instant messaging or voice or video conferences with up to 250 of your staff at a time. Lync can also be used to host meetings or webinars, even with people who don't have Lync. In your calls or meetings, you can share a digital white-board, your screen, or a particular program. Lync can retain a text transcript of your instant messenger chats in Outlook, and you can also record any of your voice or video calls to share later with people who weren't able to attend.

Lync offers presence integration with Outlook—not only can you see the current "presence status" of your contacts who are on Lync, but Lync can automatically update your own status based on your Outlook calendar.

Chapter 7

Migrating to Office 365

Once you've decided to go ahead, there are a series of steps you need to take to migrate to Office 365. The reality is that most of you will probably have an IT person or a Microsoft Partner handle the migration for you—for much the same reason that my IT firm had a lawyer create our LLC. Migration isn't alchemy, but some of the steps can be fairly technical, and it's likely that most lawyers won't want to get into the weeds with it. So in this chapter, I'm going to give you as much information as I can, but if you'd rather not know the technical details you might just want to skip to the What You Need To Know section at the end, where I'll summarize it for you at a high level.

Migration is the act of moving you from your current system to Office 365. The exact steps will vary a bit depending on what you're migrating from and which Office 365 plan you're migrating to, but I'll use this chapter to give you some general guidance on the steps involved.

I'm going to assume that you're migrating to an Office 365 plan that actually needs you to migrate data from another system. If you're just getting Office 365 ProPlus, then that's just Office 2013, and that's really more of an upgrade than a migration: for our purposes, not much different than the last time you upgraded Microsoft Office. In fact, Office 365 ProPlus is the first version of Microsoft Office that will easily coexist with a previous version of Office in the same user profile...so you not only don't have to migrate data, you don't even really have to upgrade if you want to keep both versions for some reason.

Our primary focus in this chapter will be on migrating your e-mail to Exchange Online, and I'll talk just a bit about migrating to SharePoint online as well, if you have files in your current system you want to move there.

Before you start any migration process it's a good idea to have a known-good backup of your data. That way in the unlikely event that something goes really wrong, you always know you can get your critical data back.

Also, whenever you're talking about transferring a large amount of data into or out of your office, the speed of your Internet connection becomes a big factor in the experience. Most Internet connections are advertised by download speed (i.e., 30Mbps), but frequently the Internet service provider (ISP) is less anxious to tell you what the upload speed is (i.e., 6Mbps). If your Internet connection has 6Mbps upload speeds and you have 50GB of data to push up to a Cloud server, for example, you would be looking at more than 17 hours of time to complete that transfer.

The very first step in migrating to Office 365 is getting your Office 365 account. We covered that in Chapter 2, so I'm going to assume that you've subscribed to Office 365 and you're ready to start using it.

As I mentioned in earlier chapters, it is possible to get a free, limited-time trial of Office 365. It may be tempting to migrate to the trial subscription but unless you're positive you're going to be buying Office 365 and using it as your production environment, I wouldn't do that. If you decide at the end of the trial not to continue with Office 365, you're going to find yourself having to migrate back *out* of Office 365, and that's more trouble than you want. Use the temporary accounts in the trial for testing, and wait until you're ready to move forward before you migrate any of your production domains or data to Office 365.

Before you get started, you'll want to have certain information at hand, so I recommend you get these questions answered before you start:

- Which domain names are we going to set up on Office 365? Do we already own them or do we have to acquire them?
- Where is the DNS (Domain Name System) for those domain names hosted currently? Internally? GoDaddy? Network Solutions? Elsewhere? Do we have the username and password needed to control that DNS, or are we in contact with somebody who can?
- Do we know all of the user accounts we need to create? Do we know all of the e-mail aliases (addresses) and groups that we need to create and who the members of those groups need to be?
- Are we just migrating e-mail or do we also have to migrate calendars, contacts, and tasks as well? Where is that data stored now?
- What devices do we need to connect? Outlook? PC or Mac? What version? Everybody on at least 2007? Mobile devices?
- Have the users been notified that the migration is going to occur?

Setting Up Your Domain

After you've subscribed to Office 365, the first step is to set-up and verify your domain with Microsoft. To verify that you own the domain name, Microsoft is going to ask you to add a single, harmless record into the DNS for your domain. It's sort of like having you verify that you own a car by asking you to produce the key and unlock it. They figure if you can change the DNS records in a particular way then you must control that domain.

Even though this step is harmless, unless you're pretty comfortable editing DNS records, you're probably better off leaving this step to your web designer, IT guy, or Microsoft Partner. DNS isn't rocket science, but it can be confusing to the uninitiated, and done wrong, it could potentially disrupt your website, e-mail, or other Internet services. Our Office 365 clients typically ask us to handle this step for them. That disclaimer offered...let me outline the steps to do it.

The preferred way to confirm ownership is to add a **TXT record** to the DNS for your domain and Microsoft will give you one with a specific value—similar to "ms=ms12345678"—for your domain.

Sign into your Office 365 portal at http://portal.office365.com with the username Microsoft gave you when you signed up (it probably looks like you@yourfirmname.onmicrosoft.com). Click **domains** in the navigation pane at the left and then click **Add a domain**. Office 365 will walk you through a series of steps. It will ask you to specify your domain name (i.e. yourfirmname.com), and then it will give you the specific steps to add the text Microsoft gave you to your DNS. The exact steps depend on which company (i.e., Network Solutions or GoDaddy or Hover or...) is hosting your DNS currently.

Follow the instructions provided to log into your DNS provider, or use the generic instructions to just obtain your customized value and add that key yourself (or ask whomever manages your website to do it). Then add that TXT record.

TXT records, as the name suggests, are merely text records. They're like adding comments. They have no technical effect, so adding this TXT record to your domain's DNS won't affect your website or your existing e-mail or anything else in your domain.

Once the TXT record is added to your domain's DNS records, it can take anywhere from a few minutes to a few hours for that change to take effect. The next step in the Microsoft wizard will ask you to click a button to verify the domain (see Figure 7.1).

Figure 7.1 Verifying You Own the Domain

If you're not able to add a TXT record, for whatever reason, Microsoft will give you a **placebo MX record** that you can enter instead, and it will serve the same purpose. MX records can have real effect in DNS, however, so I much prefer to use the TXT record option when I have the chance. Even if you make a hash of entering the TXT record, chances are the worst that can happen is that you don't successfully verify the domain name with Office 365. If you enter an MX record badly, you could affect your production e-mail delivery in a bad way.

Once you have successfully verified the domain, you can move on to the next step—adding users.

Adding Your Users to Office 365

If you're migrating from an existing Exchange Server to Office 365, you can probably skip this section and go straight to Migrating From a Previous Exchange Server under the Migrating Legacy Data section later in this chapter. If you're not migrating from an existing Exchange server...read on.

There are a few different ways you can add users to Office 365, and the method you choose depends a little on your current environment and how many users you have. If you only have five users, then save yourself a lot of hassle and just create them manually. It only takes 30 seconds or so to create each user, and there's no point making it any more complicated than it needs to be.

Simply go back to the **users and groups** section of the Office 365 portal and click the **+ sign** to add each user. We talked about some of the fine points of adding and managing users in Chapter 7 so you can refer to that if you need to...but you probably won't need to.

If you have a larger group of users and would to add them en masse, you could create a .CSV, (Comma Separated Values) file that contains your user list, and then simply upload that file. To get started on that go to **users and groups** and click the **Bulk Add** button, which is next to the plus sign. On the ensuing screen (see Figure 7.2), Office 365 will ask you to upload the .CSV file containing your user list. It can't be just any .CSV file though, it has to be in a very particular format. If you've done this before, then you already know that format, but if this is your first time, you may need a bit of guidance. Fortunately on the same screen where you can specify and upload your .CSV file, Microsoft offers you a sample .CSV file that you can download and edit in order to get the format right.

Figure 7.2 You Can Bulk-Add Users if You Have More than a Handful

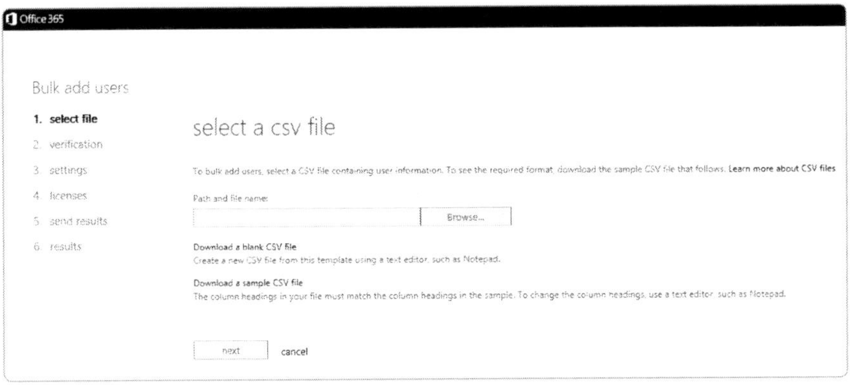

Download the sample file, and just replace the sample values with your actual user information. Figure 7.3 shows you what a sample .CSV file looks like.

Figure 7.3 Sample .CSV File

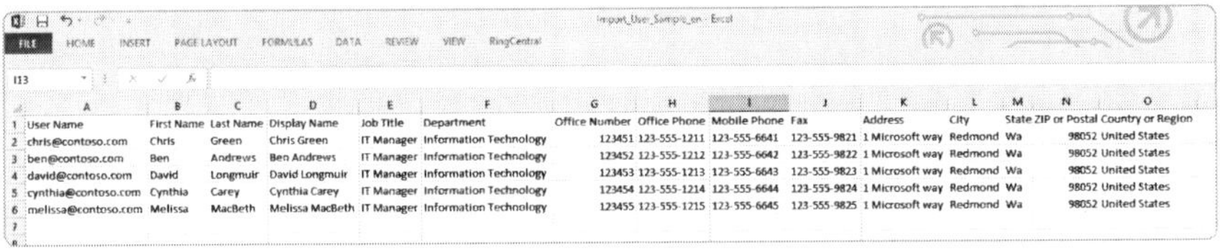

User Name	First Name	Last Name	Display Name	Job Title	Department	Office Number	Office Phone	Mobile Phone	Fax	Address	City	State	ZIP or Postal	Country or Region
chris@contoso.com	Chris	Green	Chris Green	IT Manager	Information Technology	123451	123-555-1211	123-555-6641	123-555-9821	1 Microsoft way	Redmond	Wa	98052	United States
ben@contoso.com	Ben	Andrews	Ben Andrews	IT Manager	Information Technology	123452	123-555-1212	123-555-6642	123-555-9822	1 Microsoft way	Redmond	Wa	98052	United States
david@contoso.com	David	Longmuir	David Longmuir	IT Manager	Information Technology	123453	123-555-1213	123-555-6643	123-555-9823	1 Microsoft way	Redmond	Wa	98052	United States
cynthia@contoso.com	Cynthia	Carey	Cynthia Carey	IT Manager	Information Technology	123454	123-555-1214	123-555-6644	123-555-9824	1 Microsoft way	Redmond	Wa	98052	United States
melissa@contoso.com	Melissa	MacBeth	Melissa MacBeth	IT Manager	Information Technology	123455	123-555-1215	123-555-6645	123-555-9825	1 Microsoft way	Redmond	Wa	98052	United States

Not all of the information in the sample .CSV file is required. For example, you don't have to enter an Office phone number or fax number if you don't want to. You will want to enter the user name (which conveniently is the same as a person's e-mail address), First Name, Last Name, Display Name and, interestingly, Country or Region.

Once your .CSV file is ready, select and upload it on the **select a CSV file** screen you saw in Figure 7.2, and Office 365 will create those users for you and e-mail you their temporary passwords.

With either of these first two methods of adding user accounts, Office 365 is going to give the administrator (you, presumably) temporary passwords for each of the new user accounts. Those passwords are typically in the form of "Abcd1234" where the letters and numbers are at least pseudo-random. The user (or somebody on the user's behalf) will need to log into Office 365 one time with that temporary password for Office to let the user select a real password. The easiest way to do this is for the user to sign into http://mail.office365.com with his or her username (e-mail address) and the assigned temporary password. Office 365 will automatically prompt the user to select a real password (see Figure 7.4).

Figure 7.4   Changing the User's Password

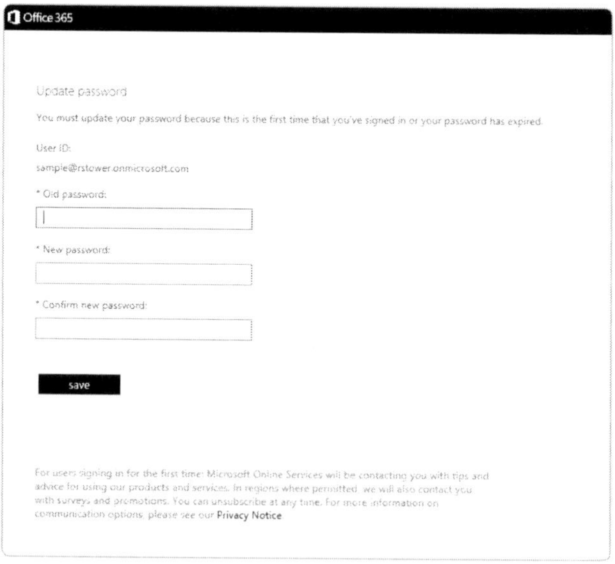

If you have a lot of users and an on-premises Active Directory (Windows Server), you might choose to create the Office 365 accounts by synchronizing your existing Active Directory accounts. There are a few advantages to doing this:

- You won't forget to add Alice from Accounting—if the user has an Active Directory (AD) account then the user will have an Office 365 account.

- Active Directory synchronization also synchronizes passwords, so the users don't have to maintain separate passwords for the local system and Office 365.

- Single sign-on—users can log into Office 365 by using their corporate credentials.

- You can manage your Office 365 accounts by using your Active Directory tools. In fact, you have to. Once you've set up Active Directory synchronization, you don't use the Office 365 portal to manage user accounts anymore.

There are a couple of downsides to using Active Directory synchronization to create your accounts as well, I suppose.

- You might accidentally add Bob, the paralegal you let go six months ago but whose Active Directory account you forgot to delete or deactivate. Setting up Active Directory synchronization does provide an excellent excuse to go through your directory and clean out any users who are no longer with you.

- Setting up Active Directory synchronization takes some prep work and will almost certainly require your IT folks to spend some time preparing for it and deploying it.

Configuring and deploying Active Directory synchronization is a bit beyond the scope of this book, but if you want the details on how to do it, Microsoft has some excellent instructions readily available, for free, on TechNet. Just Google it and you should find it quite quickly.

Creating Aliases and Groups

Once you've added the user accounts, you'll want to go back through and add any additional aliases those users need to have. Aliases are additional e-mail addresses on a mailbox for which the server will accept mail. For example: your firm administrator may have jcarter@yourfirmname.com but also accept e-mail at hr@yourfirmname.com. There's no additional charge to have multiple aliases on a mailbox. Even though they can receive e-mail from multiple addresses, only one address can be the user's default address—the address used to send new mail out. Typically that would be the primary e-mail address.

To add aliases to user mailboxes, you'll want to get into the **Exchange Admin Center**. Click **Admin** on the top navigation bar and select **Exchange** from the list of options.

You should be in the "recipients" section by default, and you should see a list of user mailboxes as you can see in Figure 7.5.

Figure 7.5   User Mailboxes

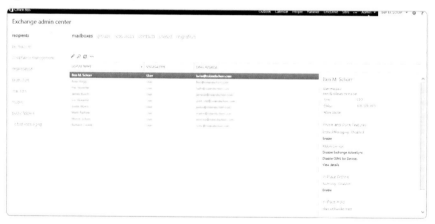

Select the mailbox to which you need to add one or more aliases, and click the **edit button** (looks like a pencil) to get the dialog box you see in Figure 7.6.

Click the **email address** link on the left side of the screen, and then click the **Add button** (looks like a + sign) to add a new e-mail address for the user. You'll need to enter the entire SMTP address (user@yourdomain.com). If you want this new alias to be the user's default e-mail address (the one that all new outgoing e-mail will come from), check the box for that before clicking **Save**.

Repeat that process for each alias and each mailbox that you need to add aliases for.

The next thing you'll want to do is create any **groups** (aka distribution lists) that you need. We talked about how to create groups in Chapter 4.

Sending As an Alias

One question that comes up occasionally is "Can I send an outgoing message as if it came from [one of my e-mail aliases]?" The answer is...if you really need to, yes.

Sending an e-mail as an alias is not officially possible, but the workaround for that is to remove the alias from the user's mailbox, then create a new distribution group with that alias as its e-mail address and make the user the only member. Give the user Send As permission on that distribution group just as above.

Figure 7.6 Editing the Mailbox Settings

Traditionally, giving a user permission to send as a group required some crafty **PowerShell** scripting, but I've recently had some success doing it through the Exchange Admin Center. Select the group the user should be able to send as, click the **edit button** (looks like a pencil), and in the

Distribution Group dialog box, click on **group delegation** on the left. Add the user to the **Send As** or **Send on Behalf** box as appropriate. Click Save.

When the user wants to send as the group, the user needs to set the From address to the group name. To do this, the user starts a new e-mail message in Outlook, goes to the **Options** tab of the **Ribbon**, and clicks **From** to turn the display of that field on, if it isn't already on. Next the user clicks the **From** button, clicks **Other email address** and enters the address of the group. Finally, the user creates and sends the message as usual. After the first time a user uses it, the group's address should appear on the list when you click the **From** field, saving a step.

Make sure that you have all of the aliases and groups in place before you move on to the next step—otherwise it's possible that some crucial mail will get missed.

The Big Change—Updating the DNS

Up to now, nothing you've done in Office 365 has really changed anything for the users (unless you've made a bad mistake somewhere). Verifying the domain, creating the users, aliases, and groups...all of that exists in a "parallel universe" that doesn't intrude on the real world of your production e-mail. This next step, however, is where things get real.

If you're migrating from an existing Exchange server, you'll want to migrate your data *before* you change your DNS records. Skip ahead a few pages to the section on migrating from a previous Exchange server, and then come back here after you've read that.

Because this step is so important, I'm going to take this opportunity once again to suggest that unless you're pretty comfortable editing DNS records, you may want to assign this task to your web designer, IT support folks, or Microsoft Partners. It's really important that this step get done correctly.

When you verify your domain name(s) in Office 365, Microsoft will give you several additional DNS records that you will need to insert in your domain's DNS when you're ready to proceed. At a minimum, it will include an **MX (Mail Exchanger) record**, a **CNAME record for AutoDiscover**, another **TXT record** (this one is for SPF) and maybe a few others as well. The proper creation of these DNS records is essential to the proper operation of Office 365, so take care to create the record correctly and without typos.

When you implement these DNS entries, especially the MX record, your e-mail will start to get diverted to Office 365. Your migration is officially underway at this point. It can take as long as 36 hours or so for the records to propagate throughout the Internet so we like to do this step late in the day on a Friday, that way the propagation can occur over the weekend, when a little disruption of e-mail service is usually tolerable. By Sunday afternoon, the changes are usually fully implemented, and we're ready to move forward.

Let's take a quick look at each of the key DNS records:

The MX Record

This record determines where your e-mail goes. After you verified your domain name ownership (as previously discussed), Microsoft gave you the exact value that you need to enter for the new MX record. It will look something like "yourfirmname-com.mail.protection.outlook.com." When you first go to edit your DNS, unless this is a brand-new domain that you haven't been receiving mail for before, you should see an existing MX record. You can delete that record and replace it with the one from Office 365 (we usually do) or you can leave that record intact and add the Office 365 record.

Some firms like to leave their old MX record in place (and their old e-mail server running) as a backup in case Office 365 goes offline for some reason. In practice, Office 365 outages are fairly rare, and getting your mail from that backup server is almost never as easy as you expect it will be. That said, if you feel safer leaving the old MX record in place as a backup, you can.

Understand that if you leave that record there, you will need to make sure it has a higher priority value than the Office 365 record. When you add an MX record, one of the required fields the DNS server is going to ask for is **Priority** (some servers call it **Cost**).

So if your existing record has a priority of 10, you need to add the Office 365 record with a lower priority value; typically we'd use 5. It's a bit counter-intuitive but the record with the lowest value in the Priority column is the one that gets tried first when a server is trying to send you e-mail. You want your e-mail to go to Office 365 whenever possible—hence the lower priority value.

If your existing record has a priority of 0, you'll need to either delete it or change its priority value to something higher so you can fit the Office 365 record under it.

The AutoDiscover Record

The AutoDiscover record is a CNAME record, which means it just maps an alias to another domain name. For example, if you have multiple domain names such as "azrealestatelaw.com" and "yourfirmname.biz" and "brillianttriallawyers.info" and you want all of those domain names to just point at "yourfirmname.com" you would do that with CNAME records.

In Office 365, this is a fairly generic record, and it will almost certainly map to "autodiscover.outlook.com". As with the MX record, when you complete the domain name verification step we talked about earlier in this chapter, Microsoft will give you the exact record you're supposed to enter here. This record is important for you—it's the AutoDiscover service that makes it easy to configure your Outlook and mobile clients as we talked about in Chapter 4. If this record is missing or not correct, you may have a lot of trouble getting the Exchange clients properly set up.

The SPF Record

SPF stands for Sender Policy Framework, and it's an anti-spam measure that is used by many (but certainly not all) e-mail servers. Essentially the way it works is that when a server receives an e-mail message from you, it looks up your SPF record, which specifies which domains are authorized to send e-mail on your behalf. It compares where the message actually came from against the SPF records list of where your messages are allowed to come from as a method of preventing e-mail spoofing (or sending fake messages from a third-party server).

The SPF record is arguably the least important of the three records we're talking about here—but it's a good idea to implement it and get it right. Systems that do check SPF will be less trusting of e-mail sent with no SPF records at all and it's possible your e-mail will get flagged as potential spam. Plus it takes only seconds to create the SPF record—so do it.

Don't worry about figuring out what the right value is. Just like the MX and CNAME records, Microsoft will give you the exact SPF record you need to enter after you verify your domain name ownership.

Connecting Clients

The next step is one we talked about in Chapter 4—connecting your clients to Exchange. We don't need to repeat what we said there—you can look back at that chapter for that information. If your autodiscover record is in place and correct, setting up clients is a very easy process. For most users, this will mean setting up Microsoft Outlook on their desktops and possibly talking them through configuring one or more smartphones and tablets.

There is one caveat, however. If you're running Office 2007 or Office 2010, you'll want to run the desktop setup to enable those clients to connect efficiently to Office 365 services. To do that, log into the Office 365 web portal at http://portal.office365.com with your e-mail address and Office 365 password. Click the **settings button** at the top right and select **Office 365 options**. Click the **software link** on the left side of the screen and then click **desktop setup**. The only button on the screen is the s**et up button**. Click that, and the update will download and install.

If you're deploying a *lot* of Office 2007 or 2010 machines, you can save the update file off to your network and then create a login script that will automatically run that installer when the user logs into the machine. If you have that many machines, though, you probably have IT folks, and they should be able to sort that out for you easily enough.

Migrating Legacy Data

Getting the new mail flowing to Office 365 and getting client devices connected to it is fairly easy. The final step, getting the legacy data—those years of e-mails, appointments, and con- tacts—migrated over to Office 365 can be somewhat trickier.

There are several scenarios to consider, and possibly one or two I haven't thought of here. Let's take a quick look at some of the most common ones.

Users Already Using Outlook— Handful of Users

We have many clients who are small firms—maybe one to five users or so—who were already using Outlook when they started with Office 365. It's possible their old system was a POP3 mailbox on GoDaddy or an IMAP mailbox on Gmail. They have all of their mail, calendars, and contacts in local PST (personal storage table) files on their C: drives, and since the number of users involved is pretty small, a manual migration is a little tedious but usually the most direct route. To do a manual migration, I encourage creating a new mail profile in Outlook that contains only Office 365 (see Chapter 4 again) and then do a **File** > **Import** (exact steps vary depending upon the version of Outlook) to bring the contents of that PST file into the same folder structure in Office 365.

Quite a Few Users with IMAP Accounts

If you have more users than you'd really want to migrate manually and they happen to be migrating from an IMAP Server, you can try using Microsoft's server-side **IMAP Migration tool**. You find it in the Exchange Admin Center (Log into portal.office365.com and click **Admin** > **Exchange** at the top) in the recipients group (which is the first one). Click **migration** on the tool tabs as you see in Figure 7.7.

Figure 7.7   The Migration Tools

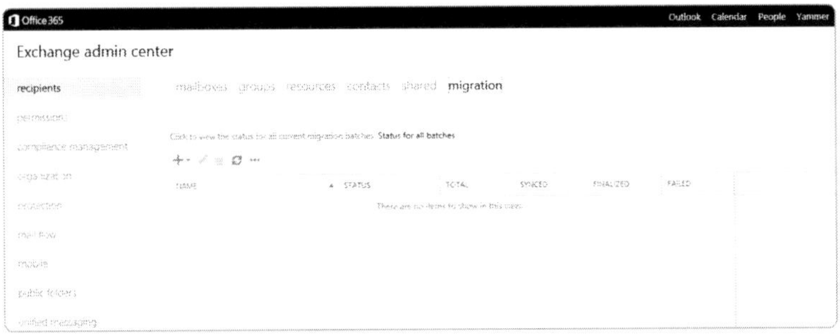

Click the **Add button** (looks like a + sign) to create a new migration batch, and select **Migrate To Exchange Online**. A wizard will start and step you through the different options. The first three options on the first screen are about migrating from existing Exchange server to Exchange online. The fourth option, however, is about migrating from an IMAP server. Select that option and click **next**.

On the next screen Exchange wants you to provide a CSV file with the mailboxes you want to migrate. The CSV file is pretty simple and can be created in Excel quite readily. It has just three field names (columns) in it:

- **EmailAddress.** The user's e-mail address in Exchange online
- **UserName.** The logon name for that user's mailbox on the IMAP server
- **Password.** The user's password on the IMAP server

Create that CSV file, with each of those field names in the header row at the top, and upload it on this screen. Then click **next**. On the next screen (see Figure 7.8), you'll get to specify the address of the IMAP server along with the authentication options. Enter that information, and then click next.

Figure 7.8   IMAP Server Address and Authentication Options

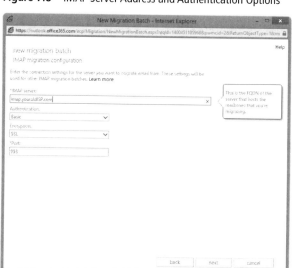

At this point, you've created a migration batch, which should start running almost immediately. It can take a little bit of time to complete, but the migration dashboard you started with in Figure 7.5 will show you the status of this (and any other) migration batches you may have running.

> Multiple batches? You might choose to create multiple migration batches if you wanted to create a test batch that just migrates a couple of users; then, once you're satisfied the test went well, you would create an additional batch or batches to migrate the rest of the users. Additionally, you might choose to stage your migration in batches, with highest priority users getting migrated first. In practice, other than test batches, I tend to just create a single batch to migrate everybody.

While the migration batches are running, the users can be using their mailboxes to send and receive mail. They'll just notice that legacy mail (and folders) will steadily populate their new mailboxes as the migration continues. Depending on the amount of legacy mail they have (and the number of mailboxes being migrated), the process could take minutes, hours or, in extreme cases, days.

Migrating From a *Previous* Exchange Server

Migrating from a previous Exchange Server is not entirely unlike an IMAP migration. Go to the migration tool in the Exchange Admin center and create a new migration batch to Exchange Online. For the type of migration, I recommend selecting a **Cutover migration**, unless you're planning to leave the old Exchange server in operation and run a hybrid environment where you're using both Office 365 and your old Exchange server.

The cutover migration assumes that you're migrating *all* of your Exchange mailboxes to Office 365, and it also assumes you have fewer than 1,000 mailboxes. Fortunately, for most law firms migrating from Exchange to Office 365, those two things are true. Also remember: the Exchange cutover migration is one in which you'll actually migrate your legacy data *before* you change your DNS records.

You need to go through a series of steps to do this kind of migration, and the steps are well-documented on Microsoft's TechNet service. You'll likely need assistance from your Microsoft Partner and/or IT support folks to get this accomplished. But if you have an existing Exchange server, you probably have those kinds of resources available to you.

When All Else Fails...

If none of those scenarios apply to you, or if you can't get the IMAP migration (for example) to work properly, third-party tools can help you to migrate your legacy mailboxes. Two of the most popular solutions are **MigrationWiz** and **Dell's Office 365 OnDemand Migration tools**.

As of this writing, each of these solutions costs between $10 and $12 per mailbox moved, and both are fairly successful at migrating mailboxes from POP/IMAP, Gmail, GroupWise, and other platforms.

If you have a large number of mailboxes to migrate, it may be worth investing in one of the third-party tools to help you with that migration, rather than toiling away with a tedious manual migration.

SharePoint

Rarely do we have to do much migration of data to SharePoint. Usually if a firm intends to use SharePoint extensively for document management, it is probably working with a SharePoint developer who will build the custom document libraries they need and handle migrating their existing documents for them.

If you just want to set up document libraries for some of your most common documents, however, there are two primary methods for migrating those to SharePoint.

Windows Explorer

If you don't have *too* many files and folders to migrate, then the easiest way is to start by creating a document library in SharePoint. Then click the **Open with Explorer** button on the **Ribbon** in SharePoint (see Figure 7.9) to open that library in Windows Explorer.

Figure 7.9 Open with Explorer

Once the library is open in Explorer, you can simply drag and drop the files and folders you need from your existing file system into the document library, and Windows will copy them over. This method is very easy, but isn't terribly robust. So if you're moving thousands of files, this is probably not the best way to go about it. But to move handfuls of files and folders, it should be perfectly capable. Keep in mind that if you move files in this way, the metadata around the file isn't preserved—things like the date the file was last modified, for example. That may or may not be an issue for you.

Third-Party Tools

Just like with Exchange migration, there are a host of third-party tools that can be used to migrate files into SharePoint document libraries. Dell has a very popular tool that can do it, and PCVita's SharePoint Migrator tool is another popular choice.

Using third-party tools has downsides: the added expense of paying for the tool, and the learning curve of figuring out how to use it, if you or your IT folks don't already have experience with it.

What You Need to Know

Migrating to Office 365 is a fairly well-established practice, though the exact steps can vary a bit depending on what you're migrating and what you're migrating from. In most cases, law firms are going to have their IT support or Microsoft Partners handle most of the technical implementation for them. It's helpful to do some reconnaissance ahead of time and make sure you have a good handle on the scope of your migration: which users you're migrating, where you're migrating from, and making sure you have all of the usernames and passwords that you need. If you've got somebody else helping to conduct the migration for you, they should have a checklist of questions to ask.

The basic steps for migration are:

1. Sign up for the Office 365 account.
2. Confirm that you own the domain name you plan to use (i.e., "MyExampleFirm.com"). Usually you'll do that by adding a text record to your domain's DNS. This can take anywhere from a few minutes to several hours, depending upon who is hosting your DNS and how responsive and smart they are.

3. Create any accounts on Office 365 that you want: janed@ myexamplefirm.com, johna@myexamplefirm.com, and so on.

4. (This is where things get real.) Update the DNS records for your personal domain, i.e., "myexamplefirm.com" to point your e-mail to the Office 365 account. This is the step you ideally want to do on a Friday afternoon. It can take as long as 72 hours for that change to propagate throughout the Internet. Once it's done, all e-mail sent to that domain will go to Office 365.

5. (You can actually do this any time after Step 1; you don't have to wait for Step 4 to complete.) If you're using Office 2007 or 2010, install the Office 365 tools on your local computer. Most of these are "behind the scenes" things that enable better SharePoint integration, and so on. Also the Lync client is part of that package. If you're on the E3 plan, this might include installing the latest version of Microsoft Office Professional Plus.

6. Set up your computer (Outlook, most likely) to access your Office 365 mailbox. Repeat for any other devices you plan to use to access the mailbox (laptops, home computer, smartphones, tablets, etc.). This is pretty easy to do and takes just a couple of minutes per device. If we did step 4 on Friday afternoon, we'd usually we do this step on Sunday afternoon or Monday morning.

7. Import your previous mail, calendar, contacts, and so on, to your new Office 365 mailbox. Depending upon the number of mailboxes involved and the type of system you're moving from, there are a few different techniques that might be used to do this.

Much of the setup of Office 365 can be done ahead of the actual migration with zero disruption to firm operations. Things get exciting when the Office 365 DNS records are finally added to your domain's DNS servers (Step 4) and then the mail starts to move to the Office 365 servers.

Like all things in the Cloud, the speed with which you can migrate and synchronize data is highly dependent on the speed of your Internet connection. Not just the download speed, but the upload speed of your connection will be a big factor.

As with all migrations, it's a good idea to have known-good backups of your data before you begin.

Chapter 8

Administration

Now that you've got Office 365, you'll have to be able to administer it. Office 365 gives you a fairly user-friendly portal that you can use to create users, reset passwords, manage licenses, and even do some of the more advanced things like basic mobile device management (MDM).

To get into that portal, open your web browser and go to http://portal.office365.com. From there, you'll be prompted to log in. Use your Office 365 username (e-mail address) and password. Once you're logged in, you should see the portal that you see in Figure 8.1.

Of course, I say you'll see the portal I show in Figure 8.1 but Microsoft has done me no favors...the portal for the Enterprise level accounts actually looks substantially different from the Small Business accounts. So the screen in Figure 8.1 is actually the portal for E-plan users. Figure 8.2 shows what the portal currently looks like for Small Business accounts.

Note: Like all things on the web, this is subject to change often and without notice. What you see on your screen right now may not be the same thing that I'm seeing when I write this book.

Figure 8.1   The Office 365 Admin Portal for Enterprise Accounts

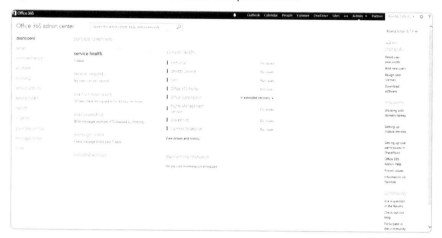

Figure 8.2   The Office 365 Admin Portal for Small Business Accounts

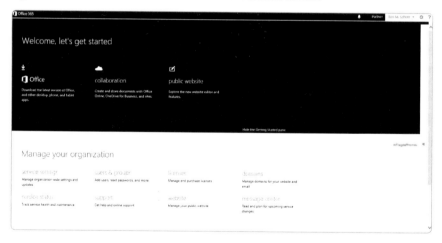

If you're ever asked by the Office 365 login process whether your account is a Microsoft Account or an Organizational Account, the answer is always **Organizational Account for Office 365** business customers. A **Microsoft Account** is the new name for what used to be called a **Live ID**, a **Microsoft Passport** or a **Hotmail** account.

Additionally, there are some advanced administration capabilities that aren't currently exposed in the web portal. To configure those settings, you have to get comfortable with PowerShell scripting, and that's way beyond the scope of this book. Your IT guy or Microsoft Partner can probably help you with that if you really need to do something that requires PowerShell.

Creating and Managing Users

In the Office 365 Portal, click the **users and groups** link to get the user list you see in Figure 8.3. The users and groups page is one of the pages you'll use most often, most likely. This is where you come to create new users or manage your existing users.

Figure 8.3 The User and Groups Page

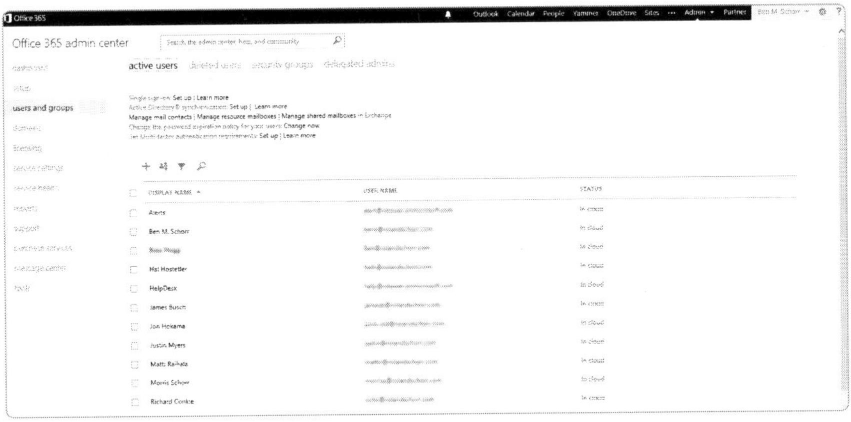

To create a new user account click the **Add button** (looks like a plus sign) to get the New user dialog you see in Figure 8.4.

Figure 8.4   The New User Dialog

Fill in the First name and Last name fields, and Office 365 will automatically generate the Display name for you—though you can certainly change it manually if you like. The user name is best set to be the user's e-mail address (ex: alice@yourfirmname. com) for simplicity. Everything under the **additional details** link is optional though you may want to fill it out if you're using things like dynamic distribution groups. Click **Next**.

On the settings page (see Figure 8.5), you can specify if the user should be an administrator or not and, if so, what kind of administrator he or she should be. For example, you might want to make your CFO the billing administrator on the account. That lets the CFO adjust account and billing settings but not other more technical settings.

Figure 8.5 The Settings Page

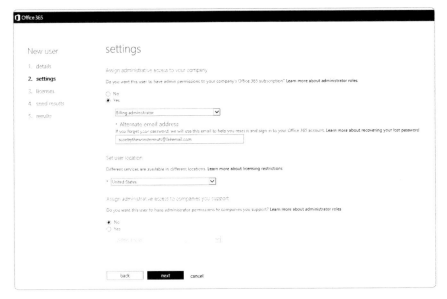

Sign-in status lets you disable an account from the user without actually deleting it or blocking it from receiving e-mail. Very few of my users bother to use this setting.

User location is important because there are different licensing and service offerings and regulations in different countries. Most, but not all, of my clients are in the United States, and in this book I've focused on those settings and services available in this country.

On the **licenses page** (see Figure 8.6) you can choose which license, or combination of licenses, the user should have. It's worth noting that you don't *have* to assign a user account any licenses—which means you can set up a user account for an administrator to manage your Office 365 without it counting against the licenses that you pay for.

Figure 8.6 The Licenses Page

The **more page** is where you can get access to advanced Exchange settings (for adding aliases and such) or advanced Lync properties specific to that user.

Resetting Passwords

Unfortunately, one of the more common administrative tasks you'll have to deal with is resetting user passwords. User passwords tend to fall into one of two camps:

- Useless but easy to remember passwords like *ABC123* or *Password1*.

- Complex things like *x8^kj34]Yy29jC* that the users forget every few days and need you to reset for them...so they can select some equally obscure and equally forgettable password to replace it.

If your users can't seem to select or remember good passphrases, perhaps you could encourage them to use a password manager like **LastPass** or **KeePass**.

Fortunately, resetting user passwords is easy enough. Sign into the Office 365 portal and go to the "users and groups" page. Find the user whose password you need to reset and click the checkbox before his or her name to select it. When you do that to the right of the user list, you'll see some options appear, as you can see in Figure 8.7.

Figure 8.7 Resetting User Passwords

	STATUS	
microsoft.com	In cloud	**Sample User**
orr.com	In cloud	sample@rstower.onmicrosoft.co
rr.com	In cloud	
orr.com	In cloud	✏ ⋮ 🗑
microsoft.com	In cloud	
chorr.com	In cloud	quick steps
schorr.com	In cloud	Reset passwords
orr.com	In cloud	
horr.com	In cloud	
chorr.com	In cloud	
orr.com	In cloud	
onmicrosoft.com	In cloud	

The first option is **Reset passwords**. Click that option and on the next screen Office 365 will ask what e-mail address(es) you want the temporary passwords sent to. If you want to send to more than one address, simply separate the addresses with semi-colons. Click the **reset password** button and Office 365 will reset the password, display the new temporary password for the account on the screen, and e-mail that temporary password to whatever addresses you specified.

The user will need to log into Office 365—such as at http://mail. office365.com—enter the temporary password (twice, actually), and select a new password.

Password Expiration

One thing that can cause users to forget their passwords often is forcing them to change their passwords too often. Either they'll forget their password or just change it to *Password2*.

To manage how often users have to change their passwords, go to the **users and groups** page in the Office 365 portal, and above the user list you'll find **Change the password expiration policy for your users** link. Click **Change Now** and you can enter the number of days before the password should expire. You can set them to expire as often as every 14 days, if you're a masochist. The maximum period you can set before expiration is 730 days. I generally recommend setting it to 365 days—though if you suspect a password has been compromised, it must be changed immediately, don't wait.

> Can I set the passwords to *never* expire? Yes, but you have to use PowerShell to do that, so it's probably a request best handled by your Microsoft Partner or IT support, unless you enjoy digging into esoteric command-line procedures.

Managing Licenses

In the course of setting up users, you may discover that you don't have enough licenses. Fortunately, that's an easy problem to resolve. In the Office 365 Admin portal, click **licensing** from the navigation pane on the left. Find the subscription that you wish to add seats to (most firms only have one kind of subscription so that might be easy), and click the name of the subscription. On the **Subscription details** page that appears, you'll see how many licenses you have now and what you're paying for that. More importantly, for our task, you'll see an **Add more** link right next to the current license count. Click that link, and you'll be taken to a page where you can specify how many additional licenses you'd like to have. Enter the quantity you want and click the **add**

licenses button. Office 365 will add the appropriate number of extra licenses to your total count and will just start charging those additional licenses to the credit card you have on the account.

Once that's done, you can return to the users and groups page, find the user(s) you wanted to add licenses for, and you should now find available licenses to assign them.

Upgrading Plans

In the early days of Office 365, switching plan families from Small Business to Midsize Business or from Midsize Business to Enterprise wasn't really possible. Well, that's not strictly true. It was possible, but to do so, you had to pull all of your data out of the existing plan, kill that plan, then start up a brand new plan and push all of your data back in. It was an annoying and time-consuming process.

Today, Microsoft has solved some of that problem. You're still not allowed to change from an Enterprise plan to a Midsize Business plan, for example, but you *can* now upgrade to a plan in a larger family—for example, from Small Business to Midsize Business or from Midsize Business to E1 (Enterprise).

To upgrade your plan, click **Admin** > **Licensing** or **Admin** > **Manage and purchase licenses**. Then on the Subscriptions page, select the plan you want to switch to, and then, under Plan options, click **Switch plans**. When you get to the **Choose a new plan page**, pick a plan, and then click **Next**. Go through the steps in the Checkout wizard, and then you can add licenses on the Review page by clicking the **Edit link** next to your new subscription.

When the **switching plans status page** appears, the switch plans process has begun and you will see this page until your plan has been switched. It's OK to close the status page and come back later; the switch will continue unabated.

Managing Anti-spam Settings

If you have an Enterprise-class plan, you have the ability to manage the spam filtering settings for your organization. To do that, click **Admin** on the top navigation bar and then select **Exchange**. In the Exchange admin center, click **protection** from the left hand navigation bar.

Malware Filter

The first tab is **malware filter**, and that sounds like it would be really interesting. Unfortunately it really isn't. Select the **default plan** and click the **edit button** (looks like a pencil) to find the limited selection of things you can configure—they're under the settings page.

First, you have the option of deleting the entire message or merely deleting the attachment when malware is detected in a message. The default is to delete the entire message, and I tend to leave it set there unless there's a good reason to change it.

The next section is a bit more useful—it lets you enable (or disable) notifications. It's possible that the person who sent the infected e-mail message doesn't realize his or her e-mail is infected. By checking one, or both, of the next two boxes you can have Office 365 send a notification message to the sender letting explaining that an e-mail message that was apparently from the sender appeared to have malware attached to it. You can even choose to customize the notification message if you really want to—though I rarely bother.

Connection Filter

Connection filtering specifies how Office 365 should treat messages originating from certain servers. Edit the default connection filter to see what settings you can configure there.

First, you can specify a whitelist of IP addresses from which Office 365 should always allow messages. Note that it only accepts IP addresses, not domain names, so if you want to whitelist your big client's mail server to make sure their messages are never filtered you'll need to know the IP address(es) of their mail server(s). Finding the IP address of a domain's mail server can be done with a combination of **NSLOOKUP** and **Ping**, though to be perfectly blunt, if you're not comfortable finding the IP address of a mail server, then you may want to rethink messing around in the Exchange Admin panel.

Below the section for whitelisting your friends and clients, is a section for blacklisting (blocking) the servers of spammers or folks you just really don't want to hear from. Just as above, this tool requires the IP address of the servers involved.

Finally, there is an unobtrusive little checkbox at the bottom of that page that tells Microsoft to go ahead and whitelist servers that have been cleared by third-party tools as being safe senders. I will almost always enable that setting to reduce the chances of false positives.

Content Filter

There are several interesting options under the **content filter** tab. First, on the **actions** page, you can specify if you want messages identified as spam to be sent to the user's **Junk Email folder** (which is the default), if you want it just passed along to the Inbox but with custom text prepended to the subject line, if you want it quarantined on the server, deleted outright, or one or two other, less interesting, options.

You can set that option differently for **spam** and for what Exchange considers **High confidence spam**, which is for the messages that seem to be really obvious spam. My preference is to have regular **spam** send to the user's Junk Email folder for review and to have **High confidence spam** quarantined on the server.

That will prevent the user's Junk E-mail folder from getting too overwhelming but at the same time give you an opportunity (for fifteen days at least) to check the quarantine if a user complains about potentially missing messages. I can't remember the last time I saw a legitimate message flagged as high confidence spam though, so the odds of ever needing to retrieve something from quarantine is pretty slim.

The **international spam** page lets you set filters that will block messages sent in certain languages (Chinese and Russian are popular choices for U.S. firms to block) or from certain countries or regions. I will block certain foreign language encodings—to be honest I can't read Korean anyhow, so I'm not likely to get any useful mail written in Korean. I tend *not* to block any countries or regions by default—there is a chance we could get a legitimate client inquiry from a foreign country (though it would have to be written in English, or maybe Spanish, for me to make much sense of it). If I start getting a lot of spam (and no legitimate messages) from a particular region or country, I may enable blocking for that country.

Exchange Server assigns a score to each incoming message, known as the **Spam Confidence Level** or **SCL**. The SCL is a number that ranges from -1 to 9. A message received from a known, trusted sender or one that was sent to a recipient address that the Exchange administrator has flagged as safe is assigned -1. Messages with a -1 aren't scanned at all; they are just passed to the Inbox. A message that is almost definitely spam and flagged as high confidence spam is assigned 9. In between those extremes, anything that scores a 5 or higher on the SCL is generally considered to be possibly spam and is likely to be placed in Junk E-mail. Anything below 5 is probably safe.

If you want to see what score a particular message got, just look at the message headers and you'll find the SCL number buried in there—usually under **X-MS-Exchange-Organization-SCL**.

The final page on the content filter we want to look at is the **advanced options** page, and there's a lot in here to look at.

The first section lets you decide when certain attributes of an incoming message will increase its spam score—or it's likelihood of being flagged as spam.

The settings you can use to adjust the spam score an incoming message receives are:

- **Image links to remote sites.** If the message is going to try to download images from remote websites, that can be an indication that it's spam. It could also be your monthly frequent flyer statement from US Airways. I generally leave this turned off.

- **Numeric IP address in URL.** Most URLs are text based (www.officeforlawyers.com, for example). If the e-mail message contains a URL with an IP address instead of text, that's a little suspicious unless you're involved in some fairly technical discussions. That doesn't make it automatically spam... but it can be suspicious. For most law firms, I turn this on.

- **URL redirect to another port.** Likewise an URL redirection to a non-standard port isn't something that most people will receive in a normal e-mail message. It's a little suspicious, so I tend to turn this on for most firms.

- **URL redirect to .biz or .info websites.** If the message contains a hyperlink to a .biz or .info site, this will increase its SCL. I tend to leave this off; I'm not convinced there aren't legitimate .biz or .info sites, though I agree that it does tend to appear more prominently in spam than in legitimate messages. Judgment call, I suppose, whether you want to enable this.

The next set of settings isn't quite so subtle. Rather than simply increasing the spam score, which *might* result in a message being marked as spam, the next group of settings will just mark a message as spam—dead stop—if the criteria are met.

- **Empty messages.** I don't get many empty messages at all, but on those rare occasions that I do it's almost always from a well-intentioned, but computer illiterate, friend. I leave this setting off.

- **JavaScript or VBScript in HTML.** This is more likely to be malware than spam, I suspect. It's not only extremely rare for legitimate messages to have script in the HTML; it's also fairly rude for somebody to embed active script in an HTML e-mail message, so I do tend to enable this setting.

- **Frame or iFrame tags in HTML.** This is fairly typical of marketing messages. Unfortunately, I also see it occasionally in messages from vendors I do work with, so I'm not willing to just mark them all as spam. The same is true of the next few settings: Object tags in HTML, Embed tags in HTML, and Form tags in HTML.

- **Web bugs in HTML.** A web bug is a graphical element, often effectively invisible to the reader, that is designed to help the sender determine if the message has been read. It's sort of a sneaky trick—I lean towards flagging messages that employ it as spam.

- **Apply sensitive word list.** Grand idea to screen messages against a list of words that would identify that message as spam. So do I enable it? No. Because not only are you prevented from editing the sensitive word list, you can't even see what's on it. I'm reluctant to flag a message as spam based on a list of words when I don't even know what's on the list.

- **SPF record: hard fail and Conditional Sender ID filtering: hard fail.** These two settings will mark as spam any e-mail message where the SPF or Sender ID test doesn't succeed. I don't have enough confidence in SPF or Sender ID to enable this setting. Yes, my domains have SPF and Sender ID. But not everybody's does, and not everybody's domain implements it correctly. I don't get a lot of spam as it is, and

I don't feel comfortable hard failing anybody's message just because the SPF might not be completely correct.

We introduced you to the SPF record in Chapter 7. It's the Sender Policy Framework record that acts as sort of a Caller ID to make it harder for spammers to spoof or fake sender addresses. Sender ID is another anti-spam technique that is occasionally used in an attempt to confirm that the claimed sender on a message is authentic.

- **NDR backscatter.** In this case, a spammer has forged one of your addresses onto its spam, and then blasted it out to a multitude of addresses. Some of those addresses are undeliverable, and the server responsible for their domain returns a Non-Delivery Report (NDR) to the apparent sender of the message. Unfortunately, the sender address was forged, so the person whose address was forged suddenly gets a flood of NDR messages for messages he or she never sent. Enabling this option attempts to prevent that. I tend not to enable it because I want to see NDR messages, and I worry that the occasional legitimate NDR will be caught. I don't begrudge those who do enable though.
- **Block all bulk e-mail messages.** This setting automatically blocks any messages that are identified as bulk e-mail (almost exclusively advertising). It's one of the few settings here that defaults to On and I recommend it.

Transport Rules

You may be familiar with using the **Rules Wizard** to create rules in Outlook to move or take action on incoming (or outgoing) e-mail that meets certain criteria. With **Exchange Transport Rules**, you can do something similar at the server level.

Want to apply disclaimers to outgoing messages automatically? Reject or delete messages that contain certain words or phrases? Get notified if any of your people send out an e-mail message containing social security numbers, bank account numbers, or other potentially sensitive information? Exchange Transport Rules can do that.

To access the Transport Rules, go into the Office 365 Admin portal, click **Admin** on the top navigation bar, select **Exchange** from the drop-down list. Click **mail flow** from the left-hand navigation pane, and on the **rules** tab, you'll find the list of your existing rules (there aren't any by default) and the tools to create new rules.

To create a new rule click the **Add button** (looks like a + sign), and start the wizard from the list that appears. If none of the template actions appeal to you, just choose **Create a new rule** from the top to the list to create something custom—like a message that blocks all incoming mail with the phrase "Help! I'm a Nigerian Prince."

Mobile Device Management

Exchange Online gives you some limited mobile device management capabilities to help you manage the wide array of mobile devices your users may be bringing into your firm. The most important settings for you to configure are found on the **mobile** page in the Exchange admin center. Click the **Admin** button on the navigation bar at the top and select **Exchange**. Click **mobile** on the left hand navigation pane, and then click **mobile device mailbox policies** at the top.

There you'll see the currently configured policies, and you can add to or edit those. Select the **Default policy** and click the **edit button** (looks like a pencil) to see the settings. On the first screen (**general**), you'll find an important checkbox—it determines whether devices that don't fully support the policies will be allowed to connect to your Exchange server anyhow. I prefer to uncheck that box to prevent old and likely less secure devices from connecting to our server.

On the **security** page you'll find the meat of this section. Let's look at the various settings:

- **Require a password.** This setting is fairly self-explanatory; will correct all those lazy users who don't want to have a password or PIN to unlock their device.
- **Allow simple passwords.** Lazy users can get a bit of an out from this setting. It lets them pick a really lame password.
- **Require an alphanumeric password.** Not too many devices support those currently, but you can check this so that devices that do support these paswords will have both letters and numbers as their password. The subsetting of this lets you specify how many different character sets (lower or uppercase characters, numbers, and symbols) to require.
- **Require encryption on device.** I always check this one; it requires the device to have at least basic encryption in order to connect.
- **Minimum password length.** With this setting, you can force at least a minimum number of characters. Without this, some users might be able to use "1" as their password. With this they'll have to use "0001" which is much better. I recommend setting this to at least 4.
- **Number of sign-in failures before device is wiped.** If the device supports this—after this number of failed sign-ins, the device will be automatically wiped clean. That's a great failsafe if you're not able to remotely wipe the device in time, and the bad guys are just guessing at the password. I usually recommend setting this somewhere between 4 and 8.
- **Require sign-in after device has been inactive for...** This setting basically lets you set the number of minutes before

an idle device will lock. I usually set it to 15 minutes. I know firms that set it to 5.

- **Enforce password lifetime.** With this setting, you can specify how many days it will be before the user is required to change their password. I often see this set to 90...I tend to turn it off. Users will tolerate having to change the passwords on their computers, but they get irritated if they have to change them on their phones, especially if the phone is their personal device. Also, since this password is only used to access the device itself, bad guys aren't sitting in a foreign country attempting to log into the user's mobile device. They have to have physical access to the device in order for this to work. That said, I won't fault you if you leave it turned on.

- **Password recycle count prevents users from reusing the same two passwords over and over.** Set the count to 5, and that means the user will have to use 5 passwords before they can reuse a password again. The truly determined user will simply change their password 6 times in 5 minutes so they can just keep the same password they had before.

When you have the settings you want, click **Save**.

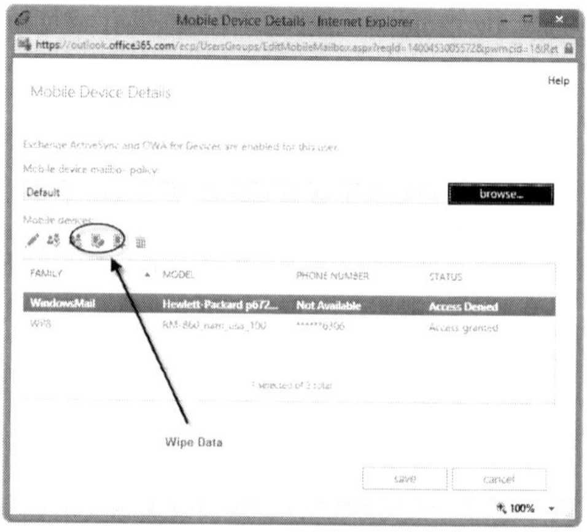

If a user loses one of his or her devices, sign into the Exchange admin center, find the user in the recipients list, and select that username. On the right side of the screen under **Phone and Voice Features**, you'll see **Mobile Devices** and below that click **View details**. Most

Figure 8.8   Remotely Wiping Missing Device

of what you see on the resulting dialog box (see Figure 8.8) is rather esoteric, but the feature you're looking for in this scenario is Wipe Data. Select the device that's gone missing and click **Wipe Data** to start that process. If you're lucky and the device is on and connected to a network, it should wipe clean.

What You Need to Know

There isn't a tremendous amount of administration that needs to be done on a daily basis, but when you do need to administer your Office 365 plan, you'll find the tools and settings you need to accomplish that in the Office 365 portal. Different plan levels (Small Business vs. Enterprise, for example) may offer different features and display them in slightly different ways. You can use the admin portal to reset user passwords, change your license count or allocation, and even configure how often users should need to change their passwords.

Office 365 hosted Exchange gives you the ability to require passwords and encryption on mobile devices that connect to Office 365 as well as to attempt to remotely wipe those devices if they go missing.

Chapter 9

Troubleshooting

Office 365 is a pretty reliable system overall, but it's not perfect. When things go wrong, there are a few steps you can take to try to right the ship.

System Health Dashboard

First, before you spend too much time chasing your tail, it's worth a visit to the System Health Dashboard. That will help you determine if the problem is on your end or if Microsoft is having a system issue on their side. If it's an issue on Microsoft's side, then there isn't much you can do other than wait for them to resolve the issue. Fortunately, such issues aren't common.

Microsoft puts a basic dashboard right on the first page of the admin portal and that looks like what you see in Figure 9.1.

Figure 9.1   The Basic Dashboard

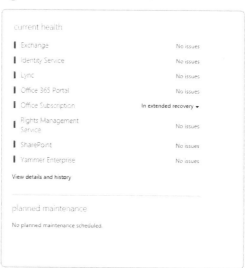

current health

▌ Exchange		No issues
▌ Identity Service		No issues
▌ Lync		No issues
▌ Office 365 Portal		No issues
▌ Office Subscription		In extended recovery ▾
▌ Rights Management Service		No issues
▌ SharePoint		No issues
▌ Yammer Enterprise		No issues

View details and history

planned maintenance

No planned maintenance scheduled.

If that dashboard doesn't prove satisfactory, you can click the **service health** link on the left side to get the more detailed dashboard like you see in Figure 9.2.

Figure 9.2   The Advanced Dashboard

If you see an issue that you'd like more information on, click it to get the dialog box you see in Figure 9.2. You'll get more details about the incident and the last updated status.

The act of checking the system health dashboard is also good for eliminating one other common cause of issues connecting to Office 365 servers—lack of Internet connectivity. If you can't get to the system health dashboard to begin with, it may be that your Internet connection isn't working properly, and that would explain why you can't get to the Office 365 servers, too.

Other Clients

The service health dashboard is very good, but it doesn't know everything. It only reflects issues that Microsoft already knows about. Another test you can do to determine if the problem is with your local machine or with the service is to try to access the service health dashboard from a different client. Try connecting from a different computer, from a mobile device, or from the web client. If it turns out you can receive Office 365 e-mail on your iPhone but not on your Mac, then the problem is with the Mac. If you can log into your SharePoint or OneDrive Pro site from another computer but not your main one, then the issue is on that computer. If you can't reach Office 365's servers from any of your devices, then the problem is likely either your network, your Internet connection, or Office 365 itself. If you can get to the Office 365 Service Health Dashboard, or Google.com, then we can probably rule out your network and the Internet...which means it would appear to be an Office 365 issue on Microsoft's end.

Updates

Some issues, especially installation or setup issues, can be caused by not having the latest updates installed. This is particularly true if you're using an older version of Microsoft Office such as 2007 or 2010.

If you're using Office 2010, you'll need to make sure you run the desktop setup, otherwise Outlook won't connect properly, and Word or Excel won't save to SharePoint properly. Log into your Office 365 portal, click the **settings button** at the top right (looks like a gear) and choose **Office 365 settings**. Click the **software** tab and run the **Desktop Setup** program you see listed there. Once that's done, reboot your computer, and try setting up Outlook or SharePoint again.

With mobile devices, having an older version of the software can leave you with occasional incompatibilities. If you're having problems, one of the first things to check is that you have the latest version of the software installed. All of the major platforms offer an easy, built-in software update capability—usually by going to the App Store for that device.

Realistically, you would have needed to run the desktop as part of your initial client setup as we described in Chapter 7. It's possible that you simply missed that step during deployment, though, so make sure it's done on this machine.

DNS Records

Another common cause for issues with Office 365—especially when you're first setting it up—is not having the DNS records correct. Microsoft will give you the exact records you need on the **domains** section. Triple-check to make sure they've been correctly configured.

One easy tool for checking these records is in the Office 365 portal itself. Log in to http://portal.office365.com and click **domains** on the left side of the screen. Click the **radio button** in front of the domain name that is having problems and click **troubleshoot** at the bottom of the screen. Microsoft will check your DNS records and tell you if, at least from their standpoint, the records are correct.

It can sometimes be helpful to see what your local DNS server thinks your DNS records look like. That can help identify issues with DNS replication or configuration that might not be obvious from looking only at the server where your DNS is hosted. One of the best tools to do that is called **NSLOOKUP**. It exists on your Windows machine as a command-line utility but if you don't feel like getting into those kinds of geek tools there is a web-based version at http://network-tools.com/nslook. Simply enter your domain name in the **Domain** field and click **Go** to get a list of the DNS records the specified DNS server thinks your domain has. If those records don't match up with what Microsoft has told you those records are supposed to be, log back into your DNS server (or ask your IT folks to) and correct the erroneous records.

We once had a client that was going to have his web guy do the DNS records. We e-mailed him all of the DNS records he needed to add, but days later it still wasn't working right. It wasn't obvious, at first glance, what was wrong. On closer inspection, we found that there was a trailing space. In other words, rather than having "them-com.eo.outlook.com" the record actually was "them-com.eo.outlook.com " with that extra space after the "m." Their web guy had copied and pasted from our e-mail and wasn't very careful to copy only the text. Once the space was removed, and an hour or three allowed for propagation, everything started working properly.

Domain Current?

Last year a client called me and said they had stopped receiving e-mail. They were still able to log into their Office 365 portal just fine, and the service health dashboard seemed fine. The problem was affecting their entire company, not just one user, and it was affecting users with mobile devices who weren't even in the same state as the office.

Oddly, it appeared that their website, which was not hosted on Office 365, was also down.

That last bit of information was the clue I needed, and the problem revealed itself quite quickly....they had forgotten to renew their domain name and it had expired. For whatever reason, their administrator had been ignoring the e-mails from their domain registrar warning that their domain was about to expire...and it did. Fortunately, it was a relatively simple matter to get their domain re-established, and by the end of the day their e-mail was flowing again.

Lesson: If your domain name expires, not only will your website disappear but your e-mail will stop flowing as well. It's a good idea to put an appointment on your calendar for a few weeks before your domain name is scheduled to expire to remind yourself to renew it.

Passwords Current?

As long as we're talking about things expiring...sometimes we see problems connecting to Office 365 when users have ignored the notices that their password was going to expire and...it did. This is particularly common for users with mobile devices that don't give them a good error message; they just fail. Have the user try logging into a different service—Outlook Web Access perhaps—using their username and what they think their password is. If it tells them their password is expired or not good, try logging into the Office 365 Admin portal and resetting their password for them.

Remember: In the Office 365 admin portal, you cannot only reset passwords, you can also control how long the users can use the same password before having to change it. I showed you how in Chapter 8.

Are You in Offline Mode?

One of the common causes for Outlook not synchronizing mail is that it's been accidentally placed in Work Offline mode. Work Offline mode is often used when the user is somewhere without Internet access (like a remote location or perhaps an airplane) and the user doesn't want Outlook to constantly, and futilely, try to synchronize with the server. Check the status bar at the bottom of the Outlook window. If it says **Working Offline** (exact text can vary slightly depending upon what version of Outlook you're using), then you're in Offline mode. Click the **Send/Receive** tab on the **Ribbon** and click the **Work Offline** button to turn Work Offline mode off.

Cached Exchange Mode

If Outlook is giving you performance problems, check to see if you're in Cached Exchange Mode. This mode is when Outlook creates a local copy of your mailbox (called an **OST file**) and then synchronizes your mailbox to that file. Everything you do in Outlook when you're in Cached Exchange Mode actually happens in that OST file. That makes Outlook faster and more stable. If you create a new appointment, Outlook writes the new appointment to that OST file. In the background, more or less constantly, Outlook will synchronize that OST file to the server (unless you're in Work Offline mode; see above), uploading your changes and downloading any new items that have arrived at the server.

One way you can tell if you're in Cached Exchange Mode is that the status bar at the bottom will say **Connected to: Microsoft Exchange** and just before that it will say **All folders are up to date** or **Updating…** followed by the name(s) of your folders. If it says **Online With: Microsoft Exchange**, then you're not in Cached Exchange Mode, and you should fix that.

The way you fix it is by going to **File > Account Settings > Account Settings**, select your Exchange account, and click **Change**. On the first screen, you should see a checkbox for **Use Cached Exchange Mode**. Check that, and then exit and restart Outlook. Outlook will create an OST file for you if you don't already have one—that's a local cache file for your entire mailbox—and it should significantly improve Outlook's performance and reliability.

Corrupted PST Files

Since you're using Office 365, you really shouldn't be making extensive use of PST files, but it's possible that you've opened some old PST files, or maybe you're using AutoArchive in Outlook and it has created some local PST files for you. If you have trouble opening those PST files or if Outlook gives you an error message stating that there is a problem with one of the PST files, you may need to run **SCANPST**.

SCANPST.EXE (aka **Inbox Repair Tool**) is a utility provided by Microsoft and automatically installed with Microsoft Outlook. Running it is fairly easy; you'll find it in the same directory that Microsoft Outlook is installed in—usually **C:\Program Files\Microsoft Office**. Double click to run it and it will ask you to select the PST file you want to test. Have it run the test. If it finds errors (see Figure 9.3), it will give you the option to back up your data file (which you should) and then click **Repair** to fix it.

Figure 9.3   SCANPST.EXE (AKA Inbox Repair Tool)

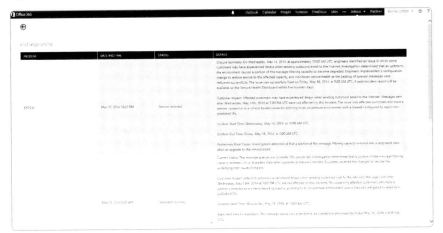

When the repair is done, SCANPST will report success. *You're NOT done!* Now you want to run **SCANPST** against that file *again*. In fact, keep running SCANPST until it gets thru the entire scan and finds *NO* errors. This could take two, three, four, or even more passes to do. If it takes ten...then you may want to just give up and restore from backups.

Once you're done, start Outlook and see if the problem is resolved.

Corrupted OST Files

If you are running Outlook in **Cached Mode** (and you should), then you will have the aforementioned OST file for your profile. Like the PST file, it's possible for the OST file to occasionally get corrupted. However, there usually isn't any point in trying to fix it. Just make sure Outlook isn't open, and delete or rename the OST file. The next time you start Outlook and connect to your Exchange server Outlook will automatically recreate a fresh OST file for you.

Additional Mailboxes

Another issue that can cause Outlook's performance to suffer is having too many additional mailboxes open in Outlook. The more load you put on your computer or on an application running on your computer, the greater the chances for performance or stability problems. Close any unnecessary mailboxes or PST files—a leaner, cleaner Outlook is a faster and more reliable one.

If you must open shared mailboxes, make sure that in **File > Account Settings > Account Settings > Exchange > Change > More Settings > Advanced** that you have the box checked to download shared folders.

While you're keeping it clean...how about emptying those 23,412 messages from your Deleted Items folder and the 7,894 from your Junk E-mail folder too? Just right-click each of those folders, and select **Empty Folder**. You can also configure Outlook to empty that folder for you automatically every time you exit Outlook. Go to **File > Options > Advanced....**

Non-Delivery Reports (NDRs)

Occasionally, when you send an e-mail message, you may get a message something like:

> Your message did not reach some or all of the intended recipients.
>
> Subject: Baker Settlement
>
> Sent: 12/11/2012 11:19 AM
>
> The following recipient(s) could not be reached:
>
> smab@boguslawfirm.com on 12/11/2012 11:19 AM
>
> The e-mail account does not exist at the organization this message was sent to. Check the e-mail address, or contact the recipient directly to find out the correct address.
>
> <server.myfirmname.com #5.1.1>

Translating these messages to figure out what went wrong can be a somewhat difficult process for the average user. But I'll spend a page or three here to help you decipher them a bit, so that you can have a good talk with your IT people about what might have happened. The first thing you need to understand is that the content of NDR messages is not standardized; it can vary a bit from server to server. Some will be fairly clear, and some will be quite esoteric.

The first thing to look at is the explanatory text, if there is any. In our sample NDR above, the explanatory text is actually quite revealing. It says rather clearly that the e-mail account does not exist at the organization the message was sent to. Generally speaking, that means that the address is probably wrong—though it could also mean that the user no longer exists. If you're sure the address is correct, it's possible that the person you're writing to no longer works there. In this case, I can see one obvious possibility for the address to be wrong. The username "smab" seems a little odd. Could it possibly be "SamB"?

Other common examples of useful explanatory text might be that the recipient's mailbox is over-quota (which means it's too full and can't accept your message right now). The message may say that the message you're trying to send exceeds their maximum message limit—which means that you need to find some way to reduce the size of your message. Most likely your message is too large due to one or more attachments. Or, perhaps it says that your message has been rejected by their spam filter, in which case, you may need to consult with their mail administrator to see how you can resolve that issue.

If the explanatory text is not useful, the next thing to look at is the three-digit code toward the end of the message. If the code begins with a *4* (such as #4.2.2), that generally means a temporary condition has stymied your message delivery. Some examples of that could be that the recipient's mailbox is full, their server is out of disk space, their server is not accepting e-mail messages at the moment, or some other similar issue. If the code begins with a 5 (such as #5.2.3), then the problem is usually more permanent. For example, #5.1.2 usually means that the domain name couldn't be resolved—which usually means that it has been mistyped in the e-mail message.

Table 9.1   A Few Common NDR Codes

The Code	What it Means
4.2.2	Recipient's mailbox is over limit.
4.3.1	There's not enough disk space on the delivery server.
5.1.1	Recipient address doesn't exist.
5.1.2	Host name can't be found. It probably means you mistyped the domain name.
5.2.x	Any 5.2.x error code will typically mean that the message is too large, probably due to one or more big attachments.
5.3.1	The code tends to mean the recipient's mail system is full.

Corrupted Profiles

Each Outlook user has a profile, which contains the customizations they've made to Outlook, the e-mail accounts they use, and other settings unique to that user. Sometimes Outlook profiles can get corrupted, in which case the easiest solution is usually to create a new one.

To create a new profile, go to **Control Panel** on the affected workstation and open the Mail applet. The result is the **Mail Setup – Outlook dialog**. Click the **Show Profiles** button and you'll get the **Mail** dialog box.

If for some reason you can't find the Mail applet, try searching for it. In Windows 7 and Windows 8, for example, there's a search box at the top right corner when you're in Control Panel. Type **Mail**, and chances are good you'll get the Mail applet in the results. If not, you may have to start it manually. To do so, go to the **C:\Program Files\Microsoft Office\Office15 folder** and look for **MLCFG32.CPL**. Occasionally, especially on Vista systems, the Mail Applet won't appear in Control Panel.

Once you've started the Mail Applet, click **Show Profiles**. From here, you can easily add a new profile by clicking the **Add** button, which will step you through the process of creating the profile, configuring the mail accounts, and specifying the default data store(s). Before you finish with this dialog box, you should check the **Prompt for a profile to be used** radio button if you're creating a second profile for testing. Next time you start Outlook, it will ask you which profile you want to start with—that makes it easy for you to test (or use) multiple profiles within the same Windows user account.

As a general rule, I would *not* delete your old profile unless you're sure you don't need it anymore. If creating the new profile doesn't resolve whatever issue you're having, you'll likely want to go back to your old profile and continue troubleshooting from there.

Repair Microsoft Office

If an Office program won't start or if it's having other problems that you can't seem to resolve, try doing a Repair install—it's a fairly harmless option that won't touch your data. To initiate it, go to **Control Panel > Add/Remove Programs** or in Vista go to **Programs and Features**. Find Microsoft Office 2013 and select **Change**. You'll get a dialog box that includes **Repair** as an option. Select **Repair** and click **Continue**. Let it run the repair—it'll check all of Outlook's program files and settings and fix any that seem to be broken. Sometimes it fixes the problem, and it rarely creates any new problems—a fairly painless thing to try. Unlike our next technique...

System Restore

This one you should check out with your IT staff or consultants (if you have any) before you try it. Vista, Windows 7, and Windows 8 all have a System Restore capability that can restore your system back to the condition it was in at a previous date. You'll find System Restore under **Start** > **Programs** > **All Programs** > **Accessories** > **System Tools**. In Windows 8, go to **Settings** > **PC Info** > **System Protection**. System Restore doesn't affect any of your data or documents; instead it restores your settings and system files back to the condition they were in on the selected date. Ideally, you would pick a date when you know the system was working fine and let System Restore try to put the computer back into that condition. If you've installed any new software or changed any settings since then, that software and those settings will likely be lost and will have to be reinstalled or reconfigured. Like I said...check with your IT guys before you do this. However, it is generally possible to un-restore if the restored condition proves unacceptable. This is a more drastic step than Repair, however, so proceed with care.

Office Safe Mode

Office can tend to accumulate a lot of add-ins and extensions to do various things like allow iTunes to synchronize your calendar. If one of the Office programs is slow or unstable, you might try starting it in Safe Mode, which disables all of the add-ins and extensions, to see if the problem goes away. To start an Office program 2013 in Safe Mode, just press and hold the **CTRL key** when you start that program. To get out of Safe Mode, just close the program and restart it normally.

Disable Add-ins

If starting in Safe Mode works, check the add-ins you have installed and disable any you don't absolutely need. To do that start the program in Safe Mode, go to **File** > **Options** > **Add-ins**, and you'll see a list of the add-ins that are installed. Click the **Go** button toward the bottom of the screen (see Figure 9.4) to get into the dialog box where you can enable or disable add-ins (see Figure 9.5). Disable everything unless you're really sure you need it, and then restart the application to see if everything's working. If that restores the application to working condition, you can try re-enabling the add-ins one-by-one until you locate the one causing the issue.

Figure 9.4 Word Options > Add-ins

Figure 9.5 Enable or Disable Add-ins

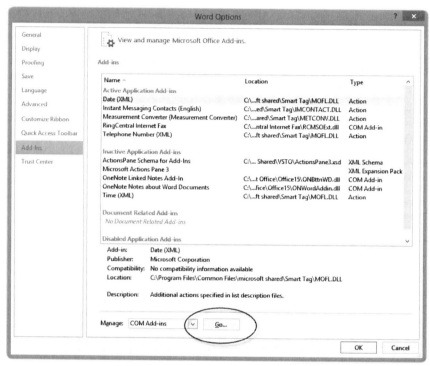

As with updates, it can also be helpful to confirm you have the latest version of any necessary add-ins. That generally means going to the vendor's website and checking to see if there's a newer version available.

Malware

Increasingly, when clients call us to report performance or reliability issues, we discover that their system integrity is compromised due to some form of malware. Make sure that your anti-virus product is up to date and operating and consider spot-checking your system with other tools like **MalwareBytes** (malwarebytes.org).

If you suspect your machine might be infected, there are also very good, free online malware scanners available from **F-Secure** and from **ESET**. Google (or Bing) **F-Secure Online Scanner** or **ESET Online Scanner**, and you'll find them easily.

Recovering from Word Crashes

If just starting Microsoft Word 2013 with a blank document causes it to crash or behave oddly, it could be that there is some corruption in your **normal.dotm**, which is the standard template that Word 2013 loads when it first starts up. Luckily this is very easy to recover from. With Word 2013 closed, locate the normal.dotm file, which should be located under **C:\Users\[your profile name]\ AppData\Roaming\Microsoft\Templates** and rename it to something like "normal.old". Then start Word normally. Word will detect that it can't find the normal.dotm file as it expected, and it will just automatically create a new one for you. If Word starts and runs normally then you can be pretty sure that the problem was some kind of corruption in your old normal.dotm file.

If Word doesn't start and run normally, then try the **Office Repair** or **System Restore** steps we talked about previously.

Additional Resources

There are a number of places you can turn for additional help with Office 365 or with the individual applications within it. One of the best is the **Office 365 for Business Community** where you can read blog articles, view free webcasts, read questions and answers from other users, and even post your own questions if necessary. You'll find the community (as of this writing) at http:// community.office365.com.

In the Office 365 portal (http://portal.office365.com), on the left side, you'll find a link to **support**. That page has a lot of information and useful links. One of those useful links is **service requests** where you can initiate a new online service request outlining your problem. In my experience, Microsoft support is fairly prompt at getting back to you on open service requests.

If you'd rather call them than open an online service request you can do that 24 x 7 x 365. The number is 1-800-865-9408. **Note**: If you're outside the USA you might have a different number. Go to the **support** section of your Office 365 portal and on the **service requests** page click **contact support**.

Your Office 365 Partner of Record

One of the best sources of support can be your Office 365 partner—if you use one. They should be familiar with how your system is configured, and you're more likely to get personal service from somebody you know—maybe even somebody located right in your own town.

If you don't have a Microsoft Partner but would like to work with one, Microsoft can introduce you to one. Check http://pinpoint.microsoft.com, a site that can help you find a local partner to work with.

What You Need to Know

Like any service, Microsoft Office 365 isn't perfect. It occasionally suffers from outages, though fortunately those outages tend to be rare. Once you've confirmed that your Internet connection is still up, check the Office 365 Service Health Dashboard in the admin portal. If it reports all of the services are normal, then it's time to troubleshoot your local machine. An Office install repair may be in order or even a system restore.

As always for best performance and maximum reliability, keep your system clean and simple. Adding a lot of unnecessary accounts or plug-ins is often a recipe for a bad experience.

Index

Page numbers followed by "f" or "t" refer to figures or tables respectively.

The Lawyer's Guide to Microsoft® Outlook 2013
By Ben M. Schorr
Product Code: 5110752 • LP Price: $41.95 • Regular Price: $69.95

Take control of your e-mail, calendar, to-do list, and more with The Lawyer's Guide to Microsoft® Outlook 2013. This essential guide summarizes the most important new features in the newest version of Microsoft® Outlook and provides practical tips that will promote organization and productivity in your law practice. Written specifically for lawyers by a twenty-year veteran of law office technology and ABA member, this book is a must-have.

Internet Legal Research on a Budget
By Carole A. Levitt and Judy Davis
Product Code: 5110778 • LP Price: $69.95 • Regular Price: $89.95

With cost-conscious clients scrutinizing legal bills, lawyers cannot afford to depend on expensive legal research databases, especially when reliable free resources are available. Internet Legal Research on a Budget: Free and Low-Cost Resources for Lawyers will help you quickly find the best free or low-cost resources online and use them for your research needs. The authors share the top websites, apps, blogs, Twitter feeds, and crowdsourced resources that will save you time, money, and frustration during the legal research progress.

The 2014 Solo and Small Firm Legal Technology Guide
By Sharon D. Nelson, John W. Simek, Michael C. Maschke
Product Code: 5110774 • LP Price: $54.95 • Regular Price: $89.95

This annual guide is the only one of its kind written to help solo and small firm lawyers find the best technology for their dollar. You'll find the most current information and recommendations on computers, servers, networking equipment, legal software, printers, security products, smartphones, the iPad, and anything else a law office might need. It's written in clear, easily understandable language to make implementation easier if you choose to do it yourself, or you can use it in conjunction with your IT consultant. Either way, you'll learn how to make technology work for you.

Entertainment Careers for Lawyers, 3rd Ed.
By William D. Henslee
Product Code: 5110769 • LP Price: $32.95 • Regular Price: $54.95

Entertainment Careers for Lawyers, Third Edition, will dispel many of the myths surrounding the practice and help lawyers and law students gain an understanding of the realities of entertainment law. Written by William D. Henslee, an experienced entertainment lawyer and law professor, this book will help you gain an overview of the substantive law areas included in entertainment law, from intellectual property and litigation to contract negotiations and estate planning. You will also earn about the career trajectories available in four major entertainment genres: music, theater, film, and television.

LinkedIn in One Hour for Lawyers, 2nd Ed.
By Dennis Kennedy and Allison C. Shields
Product Code: 5110773 • LP Price: $39.95 • Regular Price: $49.95

Since the first edition of LinkedIn in One Hour for Lawyers was published, LinkedIn has added almost 100 million users, and more and more lawyers are using the platform on a regular basis. Now, this bestselling ABA book has been fully revised and updated to reflect significant changes to LinkedIn's layout and functionality made through 2013.

Alternative Fees for Business Lawyers and Their Clients
By Mark A. Robertson
Product Code: 5110781 • LP Price: $59.95 • Regular Price: $79.95

The use of alternative fee arrangements by lawyers and the demand for those arrangements by clients is increasing. How are you and your law firm addressing this threat to the billable hour? Are you prepared to recognize that value is not measured in one-tenth-of-an-hour increments? Alternative Fees for Business Lawyers and Their Clients addresses how large firm, small firm, and solo lawyers can implement and evaluate alternative fee arrangements in transactional matters. This essential guide also provides real case studies of business lawyers and firms successfully using alternative fee arrangements to deliver value to both the clients and the lawyers.

Alternative Fees for Litigators and Their Clients
By Patrick Lamb
Product Code: 5110782 • LP Price: $59.95 • Regular Price: $79.95

Alternative Fees for Litigation Lawyers and Their Clients addresses how attorneys can implement and evaluate alternative fee arrangements in litigation matters. Written by a trial lawyer with over 30 years of experience, this essential guide offers lessons, insights, and practical tips that the author has learned during his firm's long-term experiment with alternative fee arrangements.

Personal Branding in One Hour for Lawyers
By Katy Goshtasbi
Product Code: 5110765 • LP Price: $39.95 • Regular Price: $49.95

With over 1.2 million licensed attorneys in the United States, how do lawyers stand out from their fellow practitioners and get jobs, promotions, clients, and referrals? To survive and thrive, lawyers must develop their own intentional personal brand to distinguish themselves from the competition. Personal branding expert and experienced attorney Katy Goshtasbi explains how attorneys can highlight their unique talents and abilities, manage their perceptions, and achieve greater success as a lawyer in the process.

The Lawyer's Guide to Microsoft® Word 2013
By Ben M. Schorr

Product Code: 5110757 • LP Price: $41.95 • Regular Price: $69.95

Microsoft® Word is one of the most used applications in the Microsoft® Office suite. This handy reference includes clear explanations, legal-specific descriptions, and time-saving tips for getting the most out of Microsoft Word®--and customizing it for the needs of today's legal professional. Focusing on the tools and features that are essential for lawyers in their everyday practice, *The Lawyer's Guide to Microsoft® Word 2013* explains in detail the key components to help make you more effective, more efficient, and more successful. Written specifically for lawyers by a twenty-year veteran of legal technology, this guide will introduce you to Microsoft® Word 2013.

Legal Project Management in One Hour for Lawyers
By Pamela H. Woldow and Douglas B. Richardson

Product Code: 5110763 • LP Price: $39.95 • Regular Price: $49.95

Legal clients are responding to today's unprecedented financial pressures by demanding better predictability, cost-effectiveness and communication from their outside legal service providers. They give their business to those who can manage legal work efficiently--and take it away from those who can't or won't. *Legal Project Management in One Hour for Lawyers* provides any attorney with practical skills and methods for improving efficiency, keeping budgets under control, building strong working relationships with clients, and maximizing profitability.

Adobe Acrobat in One Hour for Lawyers
By Ernie Svenson

Product Code: 5110768 • LP Price: $39.95 • Regular Price: $49.95

Most lawyers now encounter PDFs, and many own Adobe Acrobat--the most widely used software for working with PDFs. But most attorneys are confused about how to work efficiently with PDFs. *Adobe Acrobat in One Hour for Lawyers* is written for lawyers and legal professionals who want to be more organized by making better use of PDFs.

Quickbooks in One Hour for Lawyers
By Lynette Benton

Product Code: 5110764 • LP Price: $39.95 • Regular Price: $49.95

Spend more time practicing law--and less time balancing the books--by investing in easy and effective accounting software. Lynette Benton, a QuickBooks certified ProAdvisor and consultant who has helped hundreds of attorneys and small firms with financial management, will teach you to use this popular accounting software in your law practice. *QuickBooks in One Hour for Lawyers* offers step-by-step guidance for getting started with QuickBooks and putting it to work tracking income, expenses, time, billing, and much more.

WordPress in One Hour for Lawyers: How to Create a Website for Your Law Firm
By Jennifer Ellis

Product Code: 5110767 • LP Price: $39.95 • Regular Price: $49.95

Law firms without websites are placing themselves at a great disadvantage compared with the competition. Even if you feel you receive the majority of your clients through referrals, a website provides the opportunity for those potential clients to learn about you and your firm. This book will explain how to get create your firm's website quickly and easily with WordPress®software.

Twitter in One Hour for Lawyers
By Jared Correia

Product Code: 5110746 • LP Price: $24.95 • Regular Price: $39.95

More lawyers than ever before are using Twitter to network with colleagues, attract clients, market their law firms, and even read the news. But to the uninitiated, Twitter's short messages, or tweets, can seem like they are written in a foreign language. Twitter in One Hour for Lawyers will demystify one of the most important social-media platforms of our time and teach you to tweet like an expert.

Virtual Law Practice: How to Deliver Legal Services Online
By Stephanie L. Kimbro

Product Code: 5110707 • LP Price: $47.95 • Regular Price: $79.95

The legal market has recently experienced a dramatic shift as lawyers seek out alternative methods of practicing law and providing more affordable legal services. Virtual law practice is revolutionizing the way the public receives legal services and how legal professionals work with clients.

Worldox in One Hour for Lawyers
By John Heckman

Product Code: 5110771 • LP Price: $39.95 • Regular Price: $49.95

Never lose another document or waste valuable time searching for one. In just one hour, learn how to organize your documents and e-mails electronically with Worldox software. Veteran law-firm technology consult John Heckman reveals what Worldox will do for your firm--and how to customize its features for the specific needs of your practice.

PowerPoint in One Hour for Lawyers
By Paul J. Unger

Product Code: 5110705 • LP Price: $39.95 • Regular Price: $49.95

The difference between a successful presentation and an unsuccessful one can often be traced to a presenter's use--or misuse--of PowerPoint®. *PowerPoint in One Hour for Lawyers* offers practical advice for creating effective presentations quickly and easily. PowerPoint expert and attorney Paul Unger will help you avoid mishaps and develop a compelling presentation using storyboarding techniques.

Please print or type. To ship UPS, we must have your street address. If you list a P.O. Box, we will ship by U.S. Mail.

Name

Member ID

Firm/Organization

Street Address

City/State/Zip

Area Code/Phone (In case we have a question about your order)

E-mail

Method of Payment:
☐ Check enclosed, payable to American Bar Association
☐ MasterCard   ☐ Visa   ☐ American Express

Card Number   Expiration Date

Signature Required

MAIL THIS FORM TO:
American Bar Association, Publication Orders
P.O. Box 10892, Chicago, IL 60610

ORDER BY PHONE:
24 hours a day, 7 days a week:
Call 1-800-285-2221 to place a credit card order. We accept Visa, MasterCard, and American Express.

EMAIL ORDERS: orders@americanbar.org
FAX ORDERS: 1-312-988-5568

VISIT OUR WEB SITE: www.ShopABA.org
Allow 7-10 days for regular UPS delivery. Need it sooner? Ask about our overnight delivery options. Call the ABA Service Center at 1-800-285-2221 for more information.

GUARANTEE:
If—for any reason—you are not satisfied with your purchase, you may return it within 30 days of receipt for a refund of the price of the book(s). No questions asked.

Thank You For Your Order.

Join the ABA Law Practice Division today and receive a substantial discount on Division publications!

Product Code:	Description:	Quantity:	Price:	Total Price:
				$
				$
				$
				$
				$

			Subtotal:	$
**Shipping/Handling:		***Tax:**	***Tax:**	$
$0.00 to $9.99	add $0.00	IL residents add 9.25%		
$10.00 to $49.99	add $6.95	DC residents add 5.75%	****Shipping/Handling:**	$
$50.00 to $99.99	add $8.95	Yes, I am an ABA member and would like to join the Law Practice Division today! (Add $50.00)		$
$100.00 to $199.99	add $10.95			
$200.00 to $499.99	add $13.95		**Total:**	$